Copyright © 2o20 by Taj Falleni -All rights reserved.

No part of this publication may be reproduced, distributed, or transmitted in any form or by any means, including photocopying, recording, or other electronic or mechanical methods, without the prior written permission of the publisher, except in the case of brief quotations embodied in reviews and certain other non-commercial uses permitted by copyright law.

This Book is provided with the sole purpose of providing relevant information on a specific topic for which every reasonable effort has been made to ensure that it is both accurate and reasonable. Nevertheless, by purchasing this Book you consent to the fact that the author, as well as the publisher, are in no way experts on the topics contained herein, regardless of any claims as such that may be made within. It is recommended that you always consult a professional prior to undertaking any of the advice or techniques discussed within.This is a legally binding declaration that is considered both valid and fair by both the Committee of Publishers Association and the American Bar Association and should be considered as legally binding within the United States.

CONTENTS

INTRODUCTION 5
Breakfast Recipes 6
   1. Double Meat Breakfast Casserole 6
   2. Onion Tofu Scramble 7
   3. Cheesy Hash 8
   4. Bacon Veggies Combo 9
   5. Strawberries & Cream Quinoa 9
   6. Blueberry Bagels 10
   7. Blackberry Muffins 11
   8. Veggie Egg Casserole 12
   9. Cauliflower Hash Browns 13
   10. Pepperoni Omelet 14
   11. Almond French Toast 15
   12. Breakfast Stuffed Baked Potatoes 16
   13. Bacon, Tomato And Eggs 17
   14. Cherry Fritters 18
   15. Ham Spinach Ballet 19
   16. Pumpkin Spice Breakfast Cake 20
   17. Ham And Eggs Casserole 21
   18. Spinach Quiche 22
   19. Cheesy Ham & Egg Casserole 23
   20. Bacon And Egg Hash 24
   21. Walnut Date Oatmeal 25
Meat Recipes 26
   22. Beefy Stew Recipe From Persia 26
   23. Bacon Swiss Pork Chops 27
   24. Shining Dinner Meal 28
   25. Spicy Beef Jerky 29
   26. Cauliflower Corned Beef Hash 30
   27. Simple Homestyle Chicken Thighs 31
   28. Salsa Chicken Breast 32
   29. Easy Kung Pao Chicken 33
   30. St. Patty's Corned Beef Recipe 34
   31. Filet Mignon Ala Carribé 35
   32. Ham Stuffed Turkey Rolls 36
   33. Beef Roast 37
   34. Subtly Sweet Chicken Breasts 38
   35. Zesty Lamb Chops(2) 39
   36. Family Dinner Pork Shoulder 40
   37. Soy Glazed Pork Tenderloin 41
   38. Bacon Spaghetti Squash 42
   39. Chicken Meatballs Buffalo Flavored 43
   40. Italian Venison 44
   41. Keto Chicken Chili 45
   42. The Shiny Chicken Stock 46

Fish And Seafood Recipes 47
   43. Salsa Tuna Steaks 47
   44. Flavorsome Salmon 48
   45. Hearty Tilapia Bowl 49
   46. Bok Choy On Ginger-sesame Salmon 50
   47. Tomato-basil Dressed Tilapia 51
   48. Eggs 'n Smoked Ramekin 52
   49. Bbq Shrimp 53
   50. Sweet 'n Spicy Mahi-mahi 54
   51. Easy Veggie-salmon Bake 55
   52. Paprika Shrimp 56
   53. Mesmerizing Salmon Loaf 57
   54. Shrimp Magic 58
   55. Pepper Crusted Tuna 59
   56. Creamy Herb 'n Parm Salmon 60
   57. Tilapia Filet Topped With Mango-salsa 61
   58. Mexican Swordfish 62
   59. Stewed Mixed Seafood 63
   60. Pasta 'n Tuna Bake 64
   61. Miso Glazed Salmon 65
   62. Fancy "rich" Guy Smoked Lobster 66
   63. Jambalaya 67

Soups & Stews 68
   64. Chickpea And Potato Soup 68
   65. White Chicken Chili 69
   66. Verde Pork Stew 70
   67. Creamy Chicken & Mushroom Soup 71
   68. Spiced Potato-cauliflower Chowder 72
   69. Seafood Stew 73
   70. Greens & Beans Soup 74
   71. Sweet Potato 'n Garbanzo Soup 75
   72. Autumn Stew 76
   73. Sunchoke & Asparagus Soup 77
   74. Sweet Potato & Black Bean Stew 78
   75. Beefy White Cream Soup 79
   76. Lamb Provencal 80
   77. Duck Ale Chili 81
   78. Vegan Approver Tortilla Soup 82
   79. Cheesy Onion Soup 83
   80. Deliciously Traditional Clam Chowder 84
   81. Sausage & Spinach Stew 85
   82. Healthy Celery 'n Kale Soup 86
   83. Chili-quinoa 'n Black Bean Soup 87
   84. Shrimp & Mango Curry 88

Dessert Recipes 89
   85. Key Lime Curd 89

86. Nutty Cinnamon 'n Cranberry Cake 90
87. Almond Cheese Cake 91
88. Caramel Apple Chimichangas 92
89. Crème Brûlée 93
90. Vanilla Yogurt 94
91. Scrumptiously Molten Lava Cake 95
92. Almond Cake 96
93. Individual S'mores Pies 97
94. Fudge Divine 98
95. Excellent Strawberry Toast Pastries 99
96. Raspberry Mug Cake 100
97. Blackberry Brioche Bread Pudding 101
98. Banana Bundt Cake 102
99. Chocolatey 'n Peanut Butter Cakes 103
100. Chocolate Cheese Cake(2) 104

INTRODUCTION

Ninja Foodi Grill: overview

The Ninja Foodi 5-in-1 Indoor Grill is an incredible multi-purpose cooking machine. It can air fry, roast, bake, dehydrate and grill indoors. It won't do your laundry or wash your car, but it does seem to do everything else. Meats, vegetables, and even fruit come out with juicy perfection. You can also use the Ninja Foodi 5-in-1 Indoor Grill to make dried fruit and beef jerky snacks.

Ninja Foodi 5-In-1 Indoor Grill: Notable Features

This multifunctional kitchen appliance can air fry, roast, bake, dehydrate and grill indoors. The amount of smoke produced is minimal so you can use it inside a kitchen or small apartment. The Ninja Foodi comes in either back or silver, both of which look sleek and modern.

Pros

Cooks with minimal smoking
Air fry crisp
1760-watt— the same BTU as an outdoor cooking unit
Dishwasher safe components

Cons

The closed lid makes it hard to see how the food is cooking inside

Grilling Meats to Perfection

Even though it is multi-purposed, the raison d'être for this cooking machine is the grilling. The Ninja Foodi nicely sears steaks to perfection while draining away the fat. Users reported that their sirloin steaks came out perfectly seared, juicy and delectable. Hamburgers come out the best, but you will achieve the best results when steaming the meat before grilling.

With the air recirculation on, the Ninja Foodi works as an air fryer. French fries will come out soft and crispy, but with a lot less oil than a traditional deep fryer. It is an utterly convenient way to cook mahi mahi fish filets and salmon steaks. Cover yours with green onions and lemon juice to prevent them being over-dried.

With most components being dishwasher safe, cleanup will be a snap. Everything can be broken down and tossed in the lower dishwasher rack.

Roasting, Baking & Dehydrating

The Ninja Foodi excels as a vegetable roaster. Roasting zucchini, tomatoes and brussel sprouts will be effortless. The recirculating air essentially turns this grill into a convection oven.

The Ninja Foodi is excellent for dehydrating fruit. Don't know what to do with those bargain fruits you picked up at the farmer's market? Slice those extra summer fruits, toss them into the machine and save them for the winter.

Smoke Reduction

The Ninja Foodi is advertised as an indoor grill and they don't claim that it is entirely smokeless. Some people have noticed that when cooking some types of drier meats or butter some smoke did manage to escape the internal venting system. Don't get me wrong, the amount of smoke produced is significantly less than other countertop grills. Fundamental physics is at work here, and the hot gasses have to go somewhere. We don't think any design could do this job correctly. We recommend using the Ninja Foodi 5-in-1 Indoor Grill with some kind of ventilation.

Now that we have an overview of how the Ninja Foodi Grill we can dive into the sea of recipes, are you ready? Let's start!

Breakfast Recipes

1. Double Meat Breakfast Casserole

Servings: 4 -6 Servings
Cooking Time: 50 Minutes

Ingredients:

- ½ pound breakfast sausage
- 2 cups hash browns, shredded and thawed
- 4 slices bacon, chopped
- 6 eggs
- ¾ cup Velveeta, cubed
- ½ cup cheddar cheese, grated
- ½ cup mushrooms, sliced
- ¼ cup red bell pepper, chopped
- ¼ cup green bell pepper, chopped
- ¼ cup onion, chopped fine
- 2 -3 tablespoons sour cream

Directions:

1. Set the cooker to saute on med-high heat. Add the sausage and cook till brown. Remove with a slotted spoon and set aside.
2. Add bacon and cook, the remove it and set aside too. Drain all but 2 tablespoons of fat from the cooking pot.
3. Add vegetables and hash browns to the pot and cook till vegetables soften, stirring often. Stir in Velveeta cheese and continue cooking till it is melted and combined.
4. Meanwhile, in a large mixing bowl, whisk together eggs, sour cream, cheddar cheese and cooked bacon together.
5. Once the Velveeta is melted, top with sausage then pour the egg mixture over that.
6. Lock the Tender Crisp lid in place and set the temperature to 350 degrees. Bake the casserole for 35 -40 minutes or the center is set. Let rest 10 minutes before serving.

2. Onion Tofu Scramble

Servings: 4
Cooking Time: 8 Minutes

Ingredients:
- 4 tbsps. butter
- 2 blocks tofu, cubed
- Salt and black pepper
- 1 c. grated cheddar cheese
- 2 medium sliced onions

Directions:
1. Mix together tofu, salt and black pepper in a bowl.
2. Press "Sauté" on Ninja Foodi and add butter and onions.
3. Sauté for about 3 minutes and add seasoned tofu.
4. Cook for about 2 minutes and add cheddar cheese.
5. Lock the lid and set the Ninja Foodi on "Air Crisp" for about 3 minutes at 340 degrees F.
6. Dish out in a serving plate and serve hot.
- **Nutrition Info:** 184 calories, 12.7g fat, 6.3g carbs, 12.2g protein

3. Cheesy Hash

Servings: 6
Cooking Time: 30 Minutes

Ingredients:

- 6 eggs
- 4 cups riced cauliflower
- ¼ cup milk
- 1 onion, chopped
- 3 Tbsp butter
- 1 ½ cups cheddar cheese

Directions:

1. Press the saute button on your Ninja Foodi and add the butter and the onions. Cook, stirring occasionally until the onions are soft, about 5 minutes.
2. Add the iced cauliflower to the pot and stir. Turn on the air crisper for 15 minutes, turning the cauliflower halfway through.
3. In a small bowl, mix the eggs and milk together then pour over the browned cauliflower.
4. Sprinkle the cheddar cheese on top and close the lid of the Ninja Foodi for one minute to just melt the cheese. Serve while hot

- **Nutrition Info:** Calories: 291g, Carbohydrates: 8g, Protein: 18g, Fat: 22 g, Sugar: 1g, Sodium: 729g

4. Bacon Veggies Combo

Servings: 4
Cooking Time: 25 Minutes

Ingredients:
- 1 chopped green bell pepper, seeded
- 4 bacon slices
- ½ c. Parmesan Cheese
- 1 tbsp. avocado mayonnaise
- 2 chopped scallions

Directions:
1. Arrange bacon slices in the pot of Ninja Foodi and top with avocado mayonnaise, bell peppers, scallions and Parmesan Cheese.
2. Press "Bake/Roast" and set the timer to 25 minutes at 365 degrees F.
3. Remove from the Ninja Foodi after 25 minutes and dish out to serve.
- **Nutrition Info:** 197 calories, 13.8g fat, 4.7g carbs, 14.3g protein

5. Strawberries & Cream Quinoa

Servings: 3-4 Servings
Cooking Time: 8 Hours

Ingredients:
- 2 cups milk
- 1 ½ cups strawberries, halved
- 1 cup dry quinoa, rinsed
- 1 medium banana, sliced
- 2 tablespoons butter
- Honey to taste

Directions:
1. Add all ingredients to cooking pot and stir to combine.
2. Secure the lid and select slow cooking function on low heat. Cook 6 – 8 hours.
3. Serve warm topped with honey.

6. Blueberry Bagels

Servings: 4 Bagels
Cooking Time: 25 Mins

Ingredients:
- 1 cup flour
- 1 cup yogurt
- ¼ cup dried blueberries
- 2 tablespoons sugar
- 1 egg white
- 2 teaspoons baking powder
- 2 teaspoons water
- ¼ teaspoon sea salt

Directions:
1. Combine dry ingredients, except berries, in a small bowl.
2. In a medium bowl, stir together the yogurt and berries. Fold in the dry ingredients till combined.
3. Knead the dough, on a lightly floured surface, several times till it is no longer sticky. Cut it into 4 pieces and roll each piece into an 8-inch long rope.
4. In a separate small bowl, stir together the egg white and water.
5. Form a loop with each dough piece and pinch the ends together.
6. Brush with the egg white mixture and add them to the fryer basket, 2 at a time.
7. Lock the Tender Crisp lid in place and set the temperature to 330 degrees. Bake 12 minutes, then repeat with remaining bagels.
8. Serve warm or let cool and store tightly wrapped for later.

7. Blackberry Muffins

Servings: 6
Cooking Time: 25 Minutes

Ingredients:
- 8 Tbsp butter
- ½ cup Baking Stevia
- 1 egg
- 1 tsp vanilla
- 2 cups coconut flour
- 2 tsp baking powder
- 1 tsp salt
- 1 cup fresh blackberries
- ½ cup buttermilk

Directions:
1. Use an electric mixer to cream the butter and stevia together until they are light and fluffy.
2. Mix the vanilla and eggs in a small bowl then add to the mixer with the butter blend. Mix until just combined
3. In a separate bowl, toss the blackberries and ¼ cup almond flour to coat the berries.
4. Add the remaining dry ingredients to the mixer and fold together by hand. Add the buttermilk and mix until smooth.
5. Add the blackberries to the batter and mix briefly.
6. Pour the muffin batter into eight silicone muffin cups. Place the muffin cups inside the Ninja Foodi on top of a metal trivet.
7. Press the air crisp button and set the temperature to 350 degrees and program the timer to 25 minutes.
8. Once cooked, a toothpick should come out of the center of the cake cleanly. Allow to cool and serve.
- **Nutrition Info:** Calories: 285g, Carbohydrates: 2g , Protein: 6g, Fat: 17g, Sugar: 3g, Sodium: 590 g

8. Veggie Egg Casserole

Servings: 4
Cooking Time: 7 Minutes

Ingredients:
- 4 eggs
- 1 Tbsp milk
- 1 tomato, diced
- ½ cup spinach
- ¼ tsp salt
- ¼ tsp ground black pepper

Directions:
1. Prepare a baking pan that fits in your Ninja Foodi bowl by greasing the pan with butter. Set aside
2. In a medium bowl, whisk together the eggs, milk, salt and pepper and then add the veggies to the bowl and stir briefly.
3. Pour the egg mix into the prepared baking pan and lower the pan into the Ninja Foodi.
4. Set the Ninja Foodi to air crisp at 325 for 7 minutes.
5. Remove the pan of eggs from the Ninja Foodi and enjoy while hot!
- **Nutrition Info:** Calories: 78g, Carbohydrates: 1g , Protein: 7g, Fat: 5g, Sugar: 2g, Sodium: 660 g

9. Cauliflower Hash Browns

Servings: 6
Cooking Time: 30 Minutes

Ingredients:
- 6 eggs
- 4 cups riced cauliflower
- ¼ cup milk
- 1 onion, chopped
- 3 Tbsp butter
- 1 ½ cups chopped, cooked ham
- ½ cup shredded cheese

Directions:
1. Press the saute button on your Ninja Foodi and add the butter and the onions. Cook, stirring occasionally until the onions are soft, about 5 minutes.
2. Add the iced cauliflower to the pot and stir. Turn on the air crisper for 15 minutes, turning the cauliflower halfway through.
3. In a small bowl, mix the eggs and milk together then pour over the browned cauliflower.
4. Sprinkle the ham over the top of the egg mix.
5. Press the air crisp button again and set the timer for 10 minutes.
6. Sprinkle the cheddar cheese on top and close the lid of the Ninja Foodi for one minute to just melt the cheese. Serve while hot
- **Nutrition Info:** Calories: 166g, Carbohydrates: 3g, Protein: 9g, Fat: 14 g, Sugar: 1g, Sodium: 278 g

10. Pepperoni Omelet

Servings: 4
Cooking Time: 5 Minutes

Ingredients:

- 4 tbsps. heavy cream
- 15 pepperoni slices
- 2 tbsps. butter
- Salt and black pepper
- 6 eggs

Directions:

1. Whisk together the eggs, heavy cream, pepperoni slices, salt and black pepper in a bowl.
2. Press "Sauté" on Ninja Foodi and add butter and egg mixture.
3. Sauté for about 3 minutes and flip the side of the omelette.
4. Lock the lid and set the Ninja Foodi on "Air Crisp" for about 2 minutes at 350 degrees F.
5. Dish out in a serving plate and serve with low carb bread.
- **Nutrition Info:** 141 calories, 11.3g fat, 0.6g carbs, 8.9g protein

11. Almond French Toast

Servings: 4
Cooking Time: 7 Minutes

Ingredients:
- 6 eggs
- 1 cup milk
- 4 cups keto almond bread, cut in cubes
- ¼ tsp salt
- 1 tsp vanilla extract
- ½ tsp cinnamon

Directions:
1. Prepare a baking pan that fits in your Ninja Foodi bowl by greasing the pan with butter. Set aside
2. In a medium bowl, whisk together the eggs, milk, salt, vanilla and cinnamon and then add the almond bread to the bowl and stir briefly. Let sit for one hour
3. Pour the egg mix into the prepared baking pan and lower the pan into the Ninja Foodi.
4. Set the Ninja Foodi to air crisp at 325 for 18 minutes.
5. Remove the pan of French toast from the Ninja Foodi and enjoy while hot!
- **Nutrition Info:** Calories: 220g, Carbohydrates: 8g , Protein: 22g, Fat: 11g, Sugar: 5g, Sodium:708 g

12. Breakfast Stuffed Baked Potatoes

Servings: 4 Servings

Cooking Time: 8 Hours 10 Minutes

Ingredients:
- 4 potatoes, scrubbed and pricked all over
- 4 strips bacon, cooked and crumbled
- 4 eggs
- ½ cup cheddar cheese, grated
- 1 avocado, sliced
- ¼ cup chives, chopped
- 1 teaspoon olive oil
- Salt & pepper

Directions:
1. Rub the potatoes with oil and sprinkle with salt and pepper. Wrap in foil and place them in the cooking pot. Lock the lid in place and select slow cooking function on low heat. Cook potatoes overnight.
2. In the morning, carefully remove the potatoes and set the cooker to saute on med-high heat. Cook bacon till crisp, drain on paper towel and crumble when cool enough to do so.
3. Fry the eggs how you like them.
4. To assemble, cut the potatoes open, sprinkle cheese over them. Top with bacon, an egg, a slice of avocado and the chives. Salt and pepper to taste and enjoy.

13. Bacon, Tomato And Eggs

Servings: 4
Cooking Time: 7 Minutes

Ingredients:
- 4 eggs
- 1 Tbsp milk
- ½ cup crumbled bacon
- 1 tomato, diced
- ¼ tsp salt
- ¼ tsp ground black pepper

Directions:
1. Prepare a baking pan that fits in your Ninja Foodi bowl by greasing the pan with butter. Set aside
2. In a medium bowl, whisk together the eggs, milk, salt and pepper and then add the ham and cheese to the bowl and stir briefly.
3. Pour the egg mix into the prepared baking pan and lower the pan into the Ninja Foodi.
4. Set the Ninja Foodi to air crisp at 325 for 7 minutes.
5. Remove the pan of eggs from the Ninja Foodi and enjoy while hot!
- **Nutrition Info:** Calories: 157g, Carbohydrates: 2g , Protein: 11g, Fat: 12g, Sugar: 3g, Sodium: 957 g

14. Cherry Fritters

Servings: 12 Fritters
Cooking Time: 30 Minutes

Ingredients:
- 2 ¾ cups flour
- 1 ¼ cups sweet cherries, pitted and chopped
- 1 cup milk
- 1 egg
- 3 tablespoons sugar
- 2 tablespoons butter, soft
- 2 ¼ teaspoons instant yeast
- 1 teaspoon vanilla
- ½ teaspoon salt
- ½ teaspoon almond extract
- Glaze
- 1 ¼ cups powdered sugar
- 3 tablespoons milk
- 1 teaspoon vanilla extract
- ½ teaspoon almond extract

Directions:
1. Make the dough the night before. In a large bowl, mix flour, sugar, yeast and salt together. Beat in milk, butter, extracts and egg till dough forms.
2. Transfer dough to a lightly floured surface and knead about 6 minutes. Place the dough into a buttered bowl and cover with plastic. Chill overnight.
3. Next day, transfer dough to a well-floured work surface. Press into a rectangle about 12 x 8 inches. Sprinkle the cherries over the dough being sure to leave about ½ inch at the edges plain. Roll up along the widest side. Slice into 12 pieces, place on flour dusted, line cookie sheet and loosely cover. Let rise for 20-30 minutes or till double in size.
4. Lightly spray the rolls with cooking spray, then add 2 at a time to the fryer basket. Place in the cooker and secure the Tender Crisp lid. Set the temperature for 360 degrees and cook 1 -2 minutes on each side, or till they are golden brown. Remove to a wire rack and repeat with remaining rolls.
5. Whisk the glaze ingredients together in a medium bowl. Dip the top of each fritter in glaze then place back on the rack. Allow several minutes for the glaze to set before serving.

15. Ham Spinach Ballet

Servings: 8
Cooking Time: 35 Minutes

Ingredients:

- 3 lbs. fresh baby spinach
- ½ c. cream
- 28 oz. sliced ham
- 4 tbsps. melted butter
- Salt and freshly ground black pepper

Directions:

1. Press "Sauté" on Ninja Foodi and add butter and spinach.
2. Sauté for about 3 minutes and top with cream, ham slices, salt and black pepper.
3. Lock the lid and set the Ninja Foodi to "Bake/Roast" for about 8 minutes at 360 degrees F.
4. Remove from the Ninja Foodi after 8 minutes and dish out to serve.
- **Nutrition Info:** 188 calories, 12.5g fat, 4.9g carbs, 14.6g protein

16. Pumpkin Spice Breakfast Cake

Servings: 6
Cooking Time: 25 Minutes

Ingredients:
- 8 Tbsp butter
- ½ cup Baking Stevia
- 1 egg
- 1 tsp vanilla
- 2 cups almond flour
- 2 tsp baking powder
- 1 tsp salt
- 1 tsp cinnamon
- ¼ tsp nutmeg
- ¼ tsp ginger
- 1 cup pumpkin puree

Directions:
1. Use an electric mixer to cream the butter and stevia together until they are light and fluffy.
2. Mix the vanilla and eggs in a small bowl then add to the mixer with the butter blend. Ix until just combined
3. Add the remaining dry ingredients to the mixer and fold together by hand. Add the pumpkin puree and mix until smooth.
4. Pour the cake batter into your Ninja Foodi and place the lid on.
5. Press the air crisp button and set the temperature to 350 degrees and program the timer to 25 minutes.
6. Once cooked, a toothpick should come out of the center of the cake cleanly. Allow to cool and serve.
- **Nutrition Info:** Calories: 176g, Carbohydrates: 8g, Protein: 3g, Fat: 16 g, Sugar: 2g, Sodium: 127 g

17. Ham And Eggs Casserole

Servings: 4
Cooking Time: 7 Minutes

Ingredients:
- 4 eggs
- 1 Tbsp milk
- 1 cup cooked, chopped ham
- ½ cup Shredded cheddar cheese
- ¼ tsp salt
- ¼ tsp ground black pepper

Directions:
1. Prepare a baking pan that fits in your Ninja Foodi bowl by greasing the pan with butter. Set aside
2. In a medium bowl, whisk together the eggs, milk, salt and pepper and then add the ham and cheese to the bowl and stir briefly.
3. Pour the egg mix into the prepared baking pan and lower the pan into the Ninja Foodi.
4. Set the Ninja Foodi to air crisp at 325 for 7 minutes.
5. Remove the pan of eggs from the Ninja Foodi and enjoy while hot!
- **Nutrition Info:** Calories: 169g, Carbohydrates: 1g , Protein: 12g, Fat: 13g, Sugar: 1g, Sodium: 455 g

18. Spinach Quiche

Servings: 6
Cooking Time: 45 Minutes

Ingredients:

- 1 tbsp. melted butter
- 10 oz. frozen and thawed spinach
- 5 beaten eggs
- Salt and black pepper
- 3 c. shredded Monterey Jack cheese

Directions:

1. Press "Sauté" on Ninja Foodi and add butter and spinach.
2. Sauté for about 3 minutes and dish out in a bowl.
3. Add eggs, Monterey Jack cheese, salt and black pepper to a bowl and transfer into greased molds.
4. Place the molds inside the pot of Ninja Foodi and press "Bake/Roast".
5. Set the timer to 30 minutes at 360 degrees F and press "Start".
6. Remove from the Ninja Foodi after 30 minutes and cut into equal sized wedges to serve.
- **Nutrition Info:** 349 calories, 27.8g fat, 3.2g carbs, 23g protein

19. Cheesy Ham & Egg Casserole

Servings: 8 Servings
Cooking Time: 4 -8 Hours

Ingredients:
- 1 bag O'Brien potatoes, frozen
- 1 dozen eggs
- ½ pound ham, diced
- 1 cup cheddar cheese, grated
- ½ cup milk
- Salt & pepper

Directions:
1. Lightly spray the inside of the cooking pot with cooking spray.
2. Place the potatoes in the pot. Then top with ham and the cheese.
3. Beat the eggs in a large bowl. Stir in milk, salt and pepper and pour over the other ingredients.
4. Secure the lid and select slow cooker function. The casserole will be done in 4 hours on high heat or 8 hours on low.

20. Bacon And Egg Hash

Servings: 6
Cooking Time: 30 Minutes

Ingredients:

- 6 eggs
- 4 cups riced cauliflower
- ¼ cup milk
- 1 cup crumbled, cooked bacon
- 1 onion, chopped
- 3 Tbsp butter
- ½ cups cheddar cheese

Directions:

1. Press the saute button on your Ninja Foodi and add the butter and the onions. Cook, stirring occasionally until the onions are soft, about 5 minutes.
2. Add the riced cauliflower to the pot and stir. Turn on the air crisper for 15 minutes, turning the cauliflower halfway through.
3. In a small bowl, mix the eggs and milk together then pour over the browned cauliflower.
4. Sprinkle the cheddar cheese on top and close the lid of the Ninja Foodi for one minute to just melt the cheese. Serve while hot

- **Nutrition Info:** Calories: 301g, Carbohydrates: 3g, Protein: 18g, Fat: 26 g, Sugar: 1g, Sodium: 595g

21. Walnut Date Oatmeal

Servings: 2 -3 Servings
Cooking Time: 3 Minutes

Ingredients:
- 2 ¼ cups water
- 1 cup old-fashioned rolled oats
- 2 tablespoons walnuts, chopped
- 2 tablespoons dates, pitted and chopped
- ½ banana, sliced

Directions:
1. Add all ingredients to the cooking pot.
2. Secure lid and select pressure cooker setting with high pressure. Set timer for 3 minutes. When timer goes off use quick release to remove the lid. Stir and serve drizzled with honey or brown sugar.

Meat Recipes

22. Beefy Stew Recipe From Persia

Servings: 2
Cooking Time: 20 Minutes
Ingredients:
- 1 tablespoons vegetable oil
- 1 onion, chopped
- 2 cloves of garlic, minced
- ¾-pound beef stew meat, cut into chunks
- 1/2 tablespoon ground cumin
- 1/4 teaspoon saffron threads
- ½ teaspoon turmeric
- ¼ teaspoon ground cinnamon
- ¼ teaspoon ground allspice
- Salt and pepper to taste
- 2 tbsp tomato paste
- 1/2 can split peas, rinsed and drained
- 2 cups bone broth
- 1 can crushed tomatoes
- 2 tablespoon lemon juice, freshly squeezed

Directions:
1. Press the sauté button on the Ninja Foodi. Heat the oil and sauté the onion and garlic until fragrant. Add cumin, saffron, turmeric, cinnamon, and allspice. Stir in the beef and sear button for 3 minutes. Season with salt and pepper to taste.
2. Pour in the rest of the ingredients.
3. Install pressure lid. Close Ninja Foodi, press the pressure button, choose high settings, and set time to 20 minutes.
4. Once done cooking, do a quick release.
5. Serve and enjoy.
- **Nutrition Info:** Calories: 466; carbohydrates: 36g; protein: 49g; fat: 14g

23. Bacon Swiss Pork Chops

Servings: 4
Cooking Time: 23 Minutes

Ingredients:

- ½ c. shredded Swiss cheese
- 4 pork chops
- 6 bacon strips, cut in half
- Salt and black pepper
- 1 tbsp. butter

Directions:

1. Apply black pepper and salt to the pork chops generously.
2. Press "Sauté" on Ninja Foodi and add butter and pork chops.
3. Sauté for about 3 minutes on each side and add bacon strips and Swiss cheese.
4. Press "Pressure" and set the timer to 15 minutes on Medium Low.
5. Transfer the steaks in a serving platter and serve hot.
- **Nutrition Info:** 483 calories, 40g fat, 0.7g carbs, 27.7g protein

24. Shining Dinner Meal

Servings: 4
Cooking Time: 14 Minutes

Ingredients:
- 2 (12-oz.) (1½-inch thick) New York strip steaks
- 1 tsp. garlic powder
- Salt and freshly ground black pepper, to taste
- ¾ lb. asparagus, trimmed
- 1 tbsp. olive oil

Directions:
1. Season the steaks with garlic powder, salt and black pepper evenly.
2. In the pot of Ninja Foodi, place ½ C. of water.
3. In the pot, arrange the reversible rack in higher position.
4. Place the steaks over the rack. Cover the Ninja Foodi with the pressure lid and place the pressure valve to "Seal" position. Select "Pressure" and set to "High" for about 2 minutes. Press "Start/Stop" to begin.
5. Meanwhile, in a bowl, add the asparagus, oil, salt and black pepper and toss to coat well. Switch the valve to "Vent" and do a "Quick" release.
6. Once all the pressure is released, open the lid. Arrange the asparagus around the steaks. Now, close the Ninja Foodi with the crisping lid and select "Broil".
7. Set time to 12 minutes and select "Start/Stop" to begin.
8. Open the lid and transfer the steaks onto a cutting board for about 5 minutes before slicing. Cut the steaks into desired sized slices and serve alongside the asparagus.
- **Nutrition Info:** Calories: 259; Carbohydrates: 3.8g; Protein: 40.1g; Fat: 9.6g; Sugar: 1.8g; Sodium: 166mg; Fiber: 1.9g

25. Spicy Beef Jerky

Servings: 6
Cooking Time: 10 Minutes

Ingredients:
- ½ pound Beef, sliced into 1/8" Thick strips
- ½ cup soy sauce
- 2 Tbsp Worcestershire sauce
- 2 tsp ground black pepper
- 1 tsp liquid smoke
- 1 tsp onion powder
- 1 tsp cayenne pepper
- ½ tsp garlic powder
- 1 tsp kosher salt

Directions:
1. Place all the ingredients in a large Ziploc bag and seal shut. Shake to mix. Leave in the fridge overnight.
2. Lay the strips on the dehydrator trays, being careful not to overlap them.
3. Place the cook and crisp lid on and set the temperature for 135 degrees for 7 hours. Once done, store in an airtight containers.
- **Nutrition Info:** Calories: 351g, Carbohydrates: 5g, Protein: 21g, Fat: 8g, Sugar: 2g, Sodium: 1530 mg

26. Cauliflower Corned Beef Hash

Servings: 6
Cooking Time: 30 Minutes

Ingredients:
- 6 eggs
- 4 cups riced cauliflower
- 1 pound corned beef, diced
- ¼ cup milk
- 1 onion, chopped
- 3 Tbsp butter
- 2 cups chopped, cooked ham
- ½ cup shredded cheese

Directions:
1. Press the saute button on your Ninja Foodi and add the butter and the onions. Cook, stirring occasionally until the onions are soft, about 5 minutes.
2. Add the riced cauliflower to the pot and stir. Turn on the air crisper for 15 minutes, turning the cauliflower halfway through.
3. In a small bowl, mix the eggs and milk together then pour over the browned cauliflower.
4. Sprinkle the corned beef over the top of the egg mix.
5. Press the air crisp button again and set the timer for 10 minutes.
6. Sprinkle the cheddar cheese on top and close the lid of the Ninja Foodi for one minute to just melt the cheese. Serve while hot
- **Nutrition Info:** Calories: 322g, Carbohydrates: 3g , Protein: 20g, Fat: 26 g, Sugar: 1, Sodium: 1008 mg

27. Simple Homestyle Chicken Thighs

Servings: 4
Cooking Time: 14 Minutes

Ingredients:

- 4 (6-oz.) boneless skin-on chicken thighs
- 1 tbsp. extra-virgin olive oil
- 2 tsp. poultry seasoning
- 1 tsp. salt

Directions:

1. In the pot of Ninja Foodi, place 1 C. of water.
2. In the pot, arrange the reversible rack in higher position.
3. Arrange the chicken thighs over the rack, skin side up.
4. Cover the Ninja Foodi with the pressure lid and place the pressure valve to "Seal" position.
5. Select "Pressure" and set to "High" for about 4 minutes.
6. Press "Start/Stop" to begin.
7. Switch the valve to "Vent" and do a "Quick" release.
8. Once all the pressure is released, open the lid
9. Coat the chicken thighs with oil evenly and season with poultry seasoning and salt.
10. Now, close the Ninja Foodi with the crisping lid and select "Broil".
11. Set time to 10 minutes and select "Start/Stop" to begin.
12. Open the lid and serve hot.
- **Nutrition Info:** Calories: 394; Carbohydrates: 0.5g; Protein: 30.2g; Fat: 29.2g; Sugar: 0g; Sodium: 710mg; Fiber: 0.1g

28. Salsa Chicken Breast

Servings: 4 Servings
Cooking Time: 8 Minutes

Ingredients:
- 4 boneless skinless chicken breasts
- ½ cup water
- 1 cup chopped tomatoes
- ½ cup chopped onion
- 1 tbsp lemon juice
- ½ tsp salt
- ¼ tsp ground black pepper

Directions:
1. Place the chicken breast in the Ninja Foodi pot and add all the ingredients to the bowl.
2. Close the pressure seal lid and set the steamer valve to seal.
3. Cook on high pressure for 8 minutes then do a quick pressure release. Serve the chicken while hot.
- **Nutrition Info:** Calories: 271g, Carbohydrates: 5g, Protein: 53g, Fat: 2g, Sugar: 4g, Sodium: 731 mg

29. Easy Kung Pao Chicken

Servings: 2
Cooking Time: 20 Minutes

Ingredients:
- 1 tablespoon olive oil
- 1 clove garlic, minced
- 1/2 teaspoon grated ginger
- 1/2 teaspoon crushed red pepper
- 1/2 onion, chopped
- 1-pound chicken breasts, cut into bite-sized pieces
- 1/4 cup soy sauce
- 2 tbsp honey
- 2 tbsp hoisin sauce
- 1/2 zucchini, diced
- 1/2 red bell pepper, chopped

Directions:
1. Press the sauté button on the Ninja Foodi and heat the oil. Sauté the garlic, ginger, red pepper, and onion until fragrant.
2. Add the chicken breasts and stir for 3 minutes until lightly golden.
3. Stir in the soy sauce, honey, and hoisin sauce.
4. Close Ninja Foodi, press bake button, set temperature to 350 ºF, and set time to 20 minutes. Halfway through cooking time, stir and continue cooking.
5. Open the lid and press the sauté button. Stir in the zucchini and bell pepper. Allow to simmer until the vegetables are cooked.
6. Serve and enjoy.
- **Nutrition Info:** Calories: 501; carbohydrates: 29.4g; protein: 40.7g; fat: 24.5g

30. St. Patty's Corned Beef Recipe

Servings: 2
Cooking Time: 60 Minutes

Ingredients:
- 2 cloves of garlic, chopped
- 1/2 onion, quartered
- 1 1/4 pounds corned beef brisket, cut in large slices
- 3-oz. Beer
- 1 cup water
- 2 small carrots, roughly chopped
- 1 small potato, chopped
- 1/2 head cabbage, cut into four pieces

Directions:
1. In the Ninja Foodi, place the garlic, onion, corned beef brisket, beer, and water. Season with salt and pepper to taste.
2. Install pressure lid. Close Ninja Foodi, press the pressure button, choose high settings, and set time to 50 minutes.
3. Once done cooking, do a quick release. Open the lid and take out the meat. Shred the meat using fork and place it back into the Ninja Foodi.
4. Stir in the vegetables.
5. Install pressure lid. Close the lid and seal the vent and press the pressure button. Cook for another 10 minutes. Do quick release.
6. Serve and enjoy.
- **Nutrition Info:** Calories:758; carbohydrates: 45.8g; protein: 43.1g; fat: 44.7g

31. Filet Mignon Ala Carribé

Servings: 2
Cooking Time: 35 Minutes

Ingredients:
- 1 filet mignon
- ½ cup pineapple, chopped
- 1-piece bacon
- ¼ teaspoon jalapeno pepper
- 2 tablespoon red onions, chopped
- 2 cloves of garlic, minced
- 2 tablespoon coconut aminos or soy sauce
- 3 tablespoon honey
- ½ of a lime, juiced
- 1 tablespoon apple cider vinegar
- ¼ teaspoon ground ginger
- 1 teaspoon thyme
- ¼ teaspoon cinnamon
- 1/8 teaspoon ground cloves
- 1/8 teaspoon ground nutmeg
- Salt and pepper to taste

Directions:
1. Place all ingredients in the Ninja Foodi and mix well.
2. Install pressure lid. Close the lid and press the pressure button. Cook on high for 35 minutes.
3. Do natural pressure release to open the lid. Serve and enjoy.
- **Nutrition Info:** Calories: 345; carbohydrates: 42.7g; protein: 22.7g; fat: 9.2g

32. Ham Stuffed Turkey Rolls

Servings: 8
Cooking Time: 30 Minutes

Ingredients:
- 4 tbsps. fresh sage leaves
- 8 ham slices
- 8 turkey cutlets
- Salt and black pepper
- 2 tbsps. melted butter

Directions:
1. Season the turkey cutlets with salt and black pepper.
2. Roll the turkey cutlets and wrap each one with ham slices tightly.
3. Coat each roll with butter and place the sage leaves evenly over each cutlet.
4. Press "Bake/Roast" on Ninja Foodi and add turkey rolls.
5. Bake for about 10 minutes at 360 degrees F and flip the sides.
6. Bake for another 10 minutes and dish out to serve.
- **Nutrition Info:** 467 calories, 24.8g fat, 1.7g carbs, 56g protein

33. Beef Roast

Servings: 6
Cooking Time: 25 Minutes

Ingredients:
- 2 pound chuck roast
- 1 Tbsp olive oil
- 1 tsp salt
- 1 tsp ground black pepper
- 1 tsp onion powder
- 1 tsp garlic powder
- 4 cups beef stock

Directions:
1. Place the roast in the Ninja Foodi pot and season with the salt and pepper. Add the oil and then use the saute function to sear each side of the roast for 3 minutes to brown.
2. Add the beef broth, onion powder and garlic powder.
3. Close the pressure cooker lid and set the timer for high pressure, 40 minutes.
4. Once the timer has gone off, naturally release the pressure from the pot.
5. Open the lid and serve while hot.
- **Nutrition Info:** Calories: 308g, Carbohydrates: 2g, Protein: 24g, Fat: 22g, Sugar: 2g, Sodium: 1142mg

34. Subtly Sweet Chicken Breasts

Servings: 2
Cooking Time: 32 Minutes

Ingredients:
- 2 (8-oz.) frozen chicken breasts
- Salt and freshly ground black pepper, to taste
- ¼ C. honey mustard sauce
- 1 tbsp. fresh parsley, chopped

Directions:
1. In the pot of Ninja Foodi, place 1 C. of water.
2. In the pot, arrange the reversible rack in higher position.
3. Arrange the chicken breasts over the rack.
4. Cover the Ninja Foodi with the pressure lid and place the pressure valve to "Seal" position. Select "Pressure" and set to "High" for about 22 minutes.
5. Press "Start/Stop" to begin. Switch the valve to "Vent" and do a "Natural" release for about 10 minutes. Then do a "Quick" release.
6. Once all the pressure is released, open the lid
7. Coat the chicken breasts with mustard honey sauce evenly.
8. Now, close the Ninja Foodi with the crisping lid and select "Broil".
9. Set time to 10 minutes and select "Start/Stop" to begin.
10. Open the lid and serve hot with the garnishing of parsley.
- **Nutrition Info:** Calories: 499; Carbohydrates: 18.1g; Protein: 48.1g; Fat: 26.7g; Sugar: 12g; Sodium: 554mg; Fiber: 0.1g

35. Zesty Lamb Chops(2)

Servings: 4
Cooking Time: 40 Minutes

Ingredients:
- 4 (6-oz.) bone-in lamb chops
- 2 tbsp. all-purpose flour
- 4 tbsp. butter
- 1 C. picante sauce
- 3 tbsp. fresh lemon juice

Directions:
1. Coat the lamb chops with almond flour evenly and set aside.
2. Select "Sauté/Sear" setting of Ninja Foodi and place the butter into the pot.
3. Press "Start/Stop" to begin and heat for about 2-3 minutes.
4. Add the chops and cook, uncovered for about 4-5 minutes or until browned from both sides. Press "Start/Stop" to stop the cooking and stir in the picante sauce and lemon juice.
5. Cover the Ninja Foodi with the pressure lid and place the pressure valve to "Seal" position. Select "Pressure" and set to "High" for about 40 minutes.
6. Press "Start/Stop" to begin. Switch the valve to "Vent" and do a "Quick" release.
7. Once all the pressure is released, open the lid. Serve hot.
- **Nutrition Info:** Calories: 452; Carbohydrates: 6.2g; Protein: 49.1g; Fat: 24.3g; Sugar: 2.1g; Sodium: 513mg; Fiber: 0.5g

36. Family Dinner Pork Shoulder

Servings: 10
Cooking Time: 10 Minutes

Ingredients:
- 3 lb. boneless pork shoulder, trimmed and cut in 2-inch cubes
- 4 tbsp. barbecue seasoning
- 1 C. apple cider vinegar
- 1 can (6 oz.) tomato paste
- 1 (16.3-oz.) tube refrigerated biscuit dough

Directions:
1. In the pot of Ninja Foodi, place pork, barbecue seasoning and vinegar.
2. Cover the Ninja Foodi with the pressure lid and place the pressure valve to "Seal" position. Select "Pressure" and set to "High" for about 35 minutes.
3. Press "Start/Stop" to begin. Switch the valve to "Vent" and do a "Quick" release.
4. Once all the pressure is released, open the lid. Now, select "Sauté/Sear" setting of Ninja Foodi and stir in the tomato paste. Select "Md:Hi" and press "Start/Stop" to begin. Cook for about 10 minutes, stirring occasionally to shred the meat.
5. Meanwhile, tear each uncooked biscuit in 2 halves. Press "Start/Stop" to stop the cooking. Arrange the biscuit halves across the surface of the pork evenly.
6. Now, close the Ninja Foodi with crisping lid and select "Bake/Roast".
7. Set the temperature to 350 degrees F for 10 minutes.
8. Press "Start/Stop" to begin, Open the lid and serve immediately.
- **Nutrition Info:** Calories: 363; Carbohydrates: 21.9g; Protein: 39.9g; Fat: 12g; Sugar: 4.3g; Sodium: 567mg; Fiber: 1.4g

37. Soy Glazed Pork Tenderloin

Servings: 8
Cooking Time: 8 Hours

Ingredients:

- 3 lb. pork tenderloin
- 1 envelope dry onion soup mix
- Salt and freshly ground black pepper, to taste
- 3 tbsp. soy sauce
- 1¾ C. chicken broth

Directions:

1. In the pot of Ninja Foodi, place all ingredients and stir to combine.
2. Close the crisping lid and select "Slow Cooker".
3. Set on "Low" for about 8 hours.
4. Press "Start/Stop" to begin.
5. Open the lid and transfer the pork tenderloin onto a cutting board.
6. Cut into desired sized slices and serve.
- **Nutrition Info:** Calories: 276; Carbohydrates: 5.3g; Protein: 46.5g; Fat: 6.3g; Sugar: 0.6g; Sodium: 1100mg; Fiber: 0.5g

38. Bacon Spaghetti Squash

Servings: 4
Cooking Time: 25 Minutes

Ingredients:
- ½ pound bacon
- 1 whole spaghetti squash
- ¼ tsp salt
- ¼ tsp ground black pepper

Directions:
1. Place the bacon in the bottom of the Ninja Foodi and put the air crisper lid on top. Set the temperature to 400 and cook for 10 minutes or until crisped to your liking.
2. Remove the bacon, crumble and set aside.
3. Cut the butternut squash in half and place in the Ninja Foodi with the cut side facing upward. Close the pressure cooker lid and set the timer to 7 minutes on high pressure. When the timer is done, do a natural pressure release and then remove the lid.
4. Shred the spaghetti squash with two forks and then toss the spaghetti with the crisped bacon. Serve with the salt and pepper.
- **Nutrition Info:** Calories: 255g, Carbohydrates: 1g, Protein: 19g, Fat: 19g, Sugar: 5g, Sodium: 312 mg

39. Chicken Meatballs Buffalo Flavored

Servings: 2
Cooking Time: 15 Minutes

Ingredients:
- ¾-pound ground chicken
- 1/4 cup almond meal
- 1/2 teaspoon salt
- 2 cloves of garlic, minced
- 2 green onions, sliced thinly
- 1 tablespoon ghee
- 2 tablespoons coconut oil, melted
- ½ cup water
- 2 tablespoons hot sauce
- Salt and pepper to taste
- 1/2 tablespoon cornstarch + 1 tablespoon water

Directions:
1. Place all ingredients in the mixing bowl except for the hot sauce, coconut oil, and cornstarch mix.
2. Mix until well combined and form small balls using your hands. Allow to set in the fridge for at least 3 hours.
3. Press the sauté button on the Ninja Foodi and heat the oil. Slowly add the meatballs and allow to sear on all sides. Add water, hot sauce, salt and pepper.
4. Install pressure lid. Close Ninja Foodi, press the pressure button, choose high settings, and set time to 10 minutes.
5. Once done cooking, do a quick release.
6. Open the lid and press the sauté button. Stir in the cornstarch slurry and allow to simmer until the sauce thickens.
7. Serve and enjoy.
- **Nutrition Info:** Calories: 356; carbohydrates: 3g; protein: 23g; fat: 28g

40. Italian Venison

Servings: 12
Cooking Time: 12 Hours

Ingredients:
- 1 C. beef broth
- ½ C. water
- 1 (12-oz.) jar pepperoncini
- 2 packets Italian seasoning
- 1 (4-lb.) venison roast

Directions:
1. In a large bowl, add broth, water, pepperoncini and Italian seasoning and mix well.
2. Add the venison roast and coat with the marinade generously.
3. Cover the bowl tightly and refrigerate to marinate for about 8 hours.
4. In the pot of Ninja Foodi, place the venison roast with marinade.
5. Close the crisping lid and select "Slow Cooker".
6. Set on "Low" for about 12 hours.
7. Press "Start/Stop" to begin.
8. Open the lid and serve.
- **Nutrition Info:** Calories: 248; Carbohydrates: 3.2g; Protein: 45.6g; Fat: 5.1g; Sugar: 0.5g; Sodium: 590mg; Fiber: 0g

41. Keto Chicken Chili

Servings: 4 Servings
Cooking Time: 8 Minutes

Ingredients:
- 1 pound chicken breast
- 1 ½ cup chicken broth
- 2 cloves of garlic, chopped
- 1 jalapeno, seeds removed, diced
- 1 bell pepper, chopped
- ½ white onion, chopped
- ¼ cup heavy cream
- 4 oz cream cheese
- 1 tsp dried oregano
- ¼ tsp cayenne pepper
- ¼ tsp salt
- 1/8 tsp ground black pepper
- ¼ cup shredded cheddar cheese

Directions:
1. Place the chicken breast in the Ninja Foodi pot and sprinkle with the oregano, salt, cayenne and ground black pepper.
2. Add the broth, garlic, jalapeno, bell pepper and onion to the pot and close the pressure cooker lid.
3. Cook on high pressure for 10 minutes. Do a quick steam release and remove the lid.
4. Add the cream cheese and heavy cream and stir to blend.
5. Sprinkle the cheese on top of the chili and put the air crisper top on. Use the broil function to brown the cheese for 2 minutes.
- **Nutrition Info:** Calories: 448g, Carbohydrates: 9g, Protein: 38g, Fat: 31g, Sugar: 6g, Sodium: 1171 mg

42. The Shiny Chicken Stock

Servings: 4
Cooking Time: 2 Hours 10 Mins

Ingredients:
- 2 lbs. meaty chicken bones
- ¼ tsp. salt
- 3½ c. water

Directions:
1. Place chicken parts in Foodi and season with salt
2. Add water, place the pressure cooker lid and seal the valve, cook on HIGH pressure for 90 minutes
3. Release the pressure naturally over 10 minutes
4. Line a cheesecloth on a colander and place it over a large bowl, pour chicken parts and stock into the colander and strain out the chicken and bones
5. Let the stock cool and let it peel off any layer of fat that might accumulate on the surface
6. Use as needed!
- **Nutrition Info:** 51 calories, 3g fat, 2g carbs. 6g protein

Fish And Seafood Recipes
43. Salsa Tuna Steaks

Servings: 4 Servings
Cooking Time: 10 Minutes

Ingredients:
- 4 Tuna Steaks, about 2 pounds
- ½ cup water
- 1 cup chopped tomatoes
- ½ cup chopped onion
- 1 tbsp lemon juice
- ½ tsp salt
- ¼ tsp ground black pepper

Directions:
1. Place the tuna in the Ninja Foodi pot and add all the ingredients to the bowl.
2. Close the pressure seal lid and set the steamer valve to seal.
3. Cook on high pressure for 8 minutes then do a quick pressure release. Serve the tuna while hot.
- **Nutrition Info:** Calories: 165g, Carbohydrates: 4g, Protein: 24g, Fat: 3g, Sugar: 3g, Sodium: 583 mg

44. Flavorsome Salmon

Servings: 2
Cooking Time: 13 Minutes

Ingredients:
- ¼ C. soy sauce
- ¼ C. honey
- 2 tsp. rice wine vinegar
- 1 tsp. water
- 2 (4-oz.) salmon fillets

Directions:
1. In a small bowl, mix together all ingredients except salmon.
2. In a small bowl, reserve about half of the mixture. Add the salmon in remaining mixture and coat well. Refrigerate, covered to marinate for about 2 hours.
3. Arrange the "Cook & Crisp Basket" in the pot of Ninja Foodi.
4. Close the Ninja Foodi with crisping lid and select "Air Crisp".
5. Press "Start/Stop" to begin and set the temperature to 355 degrees F.
6. Set the time for 5 minutes to preheat.
7. Now, place the salmon fillets into "Cook & Crisp Basket".
8. Close the Ninja Foodi with crisping lid and select "Air Crisp".
9. Set the temperature to 355 degrees F for 13 minutes.
10. Press "Start/Stop" to begin. After 8 minutes, flip the salmon fillets and coat with reserved marinade.
11. Open the lid and serve.
- **Nutrition Info:** Calories: 299; Carbohydrates: 37.4g; Protein: 24.1g; Fat: 7g; Sugar: 35.3g; Sodium: 1600mg; Fiber: 0.3g

45. Hearty Tilapia Bowl

Servings: 2
Cooking Time: 18 Minutes

Ingredients:
- 3 C. chicken broth
- 1 C. stone ground grits
- 1 C. heavy cream
- Salt, to taste
- 2 (4-oz.) tilapia fillets

Directions:
1. In the pot of Ninja Foodi, place the chicken broth, grits, heavy cream and salt and stir to combine.
2. Cover the Ninja Foodi with the pressure lid and place the pressure valve to "Seal" position. Select "Pressure" and set to "High" for about 8 minutes.
3. Press "Start/Stop" to begin. Switch the valve to "Vent" and do a "Natural" release for about 10 minutes. Then do a "Quick" release.
4. Meanwhile, spray the tilapia fillets with cooking oil spray and then, season with salt evenly.
5. Once all the pressure is released, open the lid and stir the grits mixture.
6. Arrange a large piece of fil over grits mixture.
7. Arrange the tilapia fillets over foil in a single layer.
8. Now, close the Ninja Foodi with crisping lid and select "Air Crisp".
9. Set the temperature to 400 degrees F for 10 minutes.
10. Press "Start/Stop" to begin. Open the lid and serve the tilapia fillets with grits mixture.
- **Nutrition Info:** Calories: 679; Carbohydrates: 72g; Protein: 37.7g; Fat: 29.2g; Sugar: 1.1g; Sodium: 1300mg; Fiber: 6g

46. Bok Choy On Ginger-sesame Salmon

Servings: 2
Cooking Time: 6 Minutes

Ingredients:
- 1 tablespoon toasted sesame oil
- 1 tablespoons rice vinegar
- 2 tablespoons sear button sugar
- 1/2 cup shoyu (soy sauce)
- 1 garlic clove, pressed
- 1 tablespoon freshly grated ginger
- 1 tablespoon toasted sesame seed
- 2 green onions, sliced reserve some for garnish
- 2 7-oz salmon filet
- 2 baby bok choy washed well
- 1 teaspoon miso paste mixed with a 1/2 cup of water

Directions:
1. On a loaf pan that fits inside your Ninja Foodi, place salmon with skin side down.
2. In a small bowl whisk well sesame oil, rice vinegar, sear button sugar, shoyu, garlic, ginger, and sesame seed. Pour over salmon.
3. Place half of sliced green onions over salmon. Securely cover pan with foil.
4. On a separate loaf pan, place bok choy. In a small bowl, whisk well water and miso paste. Pour over bok choy and seal pan securely with foil.
5. Add water to Ninja Foodi and place trivet. Place pan of salmon side by side the bok choy pan on trivet.
6. Install pressure lid. Close Ninja Foodi, press manual button, choose high settings, and set time to 6 minutes.
7. Once done cooking, do a quick release. Serve and enjoy.
- **Nutrition Info:** Calories: 609; carbohydrates: 30.4g; protein: 56.0g; fat: 29.2g

47. Tomato-basil Dressed Tilapia

Servings: 2
Cooking Time: 4 Minutes

Ingredients:
- 2 (4 oz) tilapia fillets
- Salt and pepper
- 2 roma tomatoes, diced
- 2 minced garlic cloves
- 1/4 cup chopped basil (fresh)
- 1 tbsp olive oil
- 1/4 tsp salt
- 1/8 tsp pepper
- 1 tbsp Balsamic vinegar (optional)

Directions:
1. Add a cup of water in Ninja Foodi, place steamer basket, and add tilapia in basket. Season with pepper and salt.
2. Install pressure lid and place valve to vent position.
3. Close Ninja Foodi, press steam button, and set time to 2 minutes.
4. Meanwhile, in a medium bowl toss well to mix pepper, salt, olive oil, basil, garlic, and tomatoes. If desired, you can add a tablespoon of balsamic vinegar. Mix well.
5. Once done cooking, do a quick release.
6. Serve and enjoy with the basil-tomato dressing.
- **Nutrition Info:** Calories: 196; carbohydrates: 2.0g; protein: 20.0g; fat: 12.0g

48. Eggs 'n Smoked Ramekin

Servings: 2
Cooking Time: 4 Minutes

Ingredients:
- 2 eggs
- 2 slices of smoked salmon
- 2 slices of cheese
- 2 fresh basil leaves for garnish
- Olive oil

Directions:
1. Add a cup of water in Ninja Foodi and place trivet on bottom.
2. Lightly grease each ramekin with a drop of olive oil each. Spread well.
3. Crack an egg in each ramekin. Place a slice of cheese, a slice of smoked salmon, and basil leaf in each ramekin.
4. Cover each ramekin with foil and place on trivet.
5. Install pressure lid. Close Ninja Foodi, press manual button, choose low settings, and set time to 4 minutes.
6. Once done cooking, do a quick release.
7. Serve and enjoy.
- **Nutrition Info:** Calories: 239; carbohydrates: 0.9g; protein: 17.5g; fat: 18.3g

49. Bbq Shrimp

Servings: 4 Servings
Cooking Time: 12 Minutes

Ingredients:

- 1 ½ pounds Shrimp, deveined and peeled
- 1 Tbsp olive oil
- 1 tsp ground paprika
- ¼ tsp salt
- ¼ tsp ground black pepper
- 1 onion, chopped
- ¼ cup hot sauce
- 1 tsp stevia
- ¼ cup water
- 2 Tbsp vinegar

Directions:

1. Turn the Ninja Foodi on to saute and add the olive oil. Once hot, add the shrimp and sear on each side for 2 minutes.
2. Sprinkle the salt and pepper on the shrimp and then add all the remaining ingredients to the pot.
3. Cover the Foodi and use the pressure cooker function to cook the shrimp for 8 minutes under high heat pressure.
4. Release the pressure using a natural steam and serve warm or chilled
- **Nutrition Info:** Calories: 207g, Carbohydrates: 1g, Protein: 36g, Fat: 6g, Sugar: 2g, Sodium: 3633mg

50. Sweet 'n Spicy Mahi-mahi

Servings: 2
Cooking Time: 10 Minutes

Ingredients:

- 2 6-oz mahi-mahi fillets
- Salt, to taste
- Black pepper, to taste
- 1-2 cloves garlic, minced or crushed
- 1" piece ginger, finely grated
- ½ lime, juiced
- 2 tablespoons honey
- 1 tablespoon nanami togarashi
- 2 tablespoons sriracha
- 1 tablespoon orange juice

Directions:

1. In a heatproof dish that fits inside the Ninja Foodi, mix well orange juice, sriracha, nanami togarashi, honey lime juice, ginger, and garlic.
2. Season mahi-mahi with pepper and salt. Place in bowl of sauce and cover well in sauce. Seal dish securely with foil.
3. Install pressure lid and place valve to vent position.
4. Add a cup of water in Ninja Foodi, place trivet, and add dish of mahi-mahi on trivet.
5. Close Ninja Foodi, press steam button and set time to 10 minutes.
6. Once done cooking, do a quick release.
7. Serve and enjoy.
- **Nutrition Info:** Calories: 200; carbohydrates: 20.1g; protein: 28.1g; fat: 0.8g

51. Easy Veggie-salmon Bake

Servings: 2
Cooking Time: 20 Minutes

Ingredients:
- 1 cup chicken broth
- 1 cup milk
- 1 salmon filet
- 2 tbsp olive oil
- Ground pepper to taste
- 1 tsp minced garlic
- 1 cup frozen vegetables
- 1/2 can of cream of celery soup
- ¼ tsp dill
- ¼ tsp cilantro
- 1 tsp Italian spice
- 1 tsp poultry seasoning
- 1 tbsp ground parmesan

Directions:
1. Press sauté button and heat oil.
2. Add the salmon and cook until white on both sides and defrosted enough to split apart, around 2 minutes per side.
3. Add the garlic and just stir into the oil then deglaze the pot with the broth for 3 minutes.
4. Add the spices, milk, vegetables, noodles and stir.
5. Add the cream of celery soup on top and just gently stir so it is mixed in enough on top to not be clumpy.
6. Install pressure lid. Close Ninja Foodi, press pressure cook button, choose high settings, and set time to 8 minutes.
7. Once done cooking, do a quick release.
8. Serve and enjoy with a sprinkle of parmesan.
- **Nutrition Info:** Calories: 616; carbohydrates: 28.7g; protein: 51.8g; fat: 32.6g

52. Paprika Shrimp

Servings: 3
Cooking Time: 20 Minutes

Ingredients:
- 1 tsp. paprika, smoked
- 3 tbsps. butter
- 1 lb. tiger shrimps
- Salt

Directions:
1. In a bowl, mix all the above ingredients and marinate the shrimps in it.
2. Grease the pot of Ninja Foodi with butter and transfer the seasoned shrimps in it.
3. Press "Bake/Roast" and set the timer to 15 minutes at 355 degrees F.
4. Dish out shrimps from the Ninja Foodi and serve.
- **Nutrition Info:** 173 calories, 8.3g fat, 0.1g carbs, 23.8g protein

53. Mesmerizing Salmon Loaf

Servings: 6
Cooking Time: 6 Hours 10 Mins

Ingredients:
- 2 slightly beaten eggs
- 1 c. chicken broth
- ¼ c. shredded cheddar cheese
- 2 c. stuffing croutons, seasoned
- 7 oz. drained salmon, skinless and boneless

Directions:
1. Mix all the ingredients except salmon in a bowl then add salmon and combine it well
2. Spray the inside of the Ninja Foodi with cooking spray
3. Make it into a loaf shape
4. Cook for 4-6 hours on low heat
5. Serve and enjoy!
- **Nutrition Info:** 220 calories, 5g fat, 13g carbs, 20g protein

54. Shrimp Magic

Servings: 3
Cooking Time: 25 Minutes

Ingredients:
- 2 tbsps. butter
- ½ tsp. paprika, smoked
- 1 lb. deveined shrimps, peeled
- Lemongrass stalks
- 1 chopped red chili pepper, seeded

Directions:
1. In a bowl, combine all the ingredients except lemongrass and marinate for about 1 hour.
2. Press "Bake/Roast" and set the timer to 15 minutes at 345 degrees F.
3. Bake for about 15 minutes and dish out the fillets.
- **Nutrition Info:** 251 calories, 10.3g fat, 3g carbs, 34.6g protein

55. Pepper Crusted Tuna

Servings: 2 Servings
Cooking Time: 5 Minutes

Ingredients:
- ½ cup water
- 2 Tbsp butter
- 1/3 cup lemon juice
- 1 pound Tuna Filets
- T tsp black peppercorns, crushed

Directions:
1. Rub the tuna with the black pepper and then place in the air crisper basket.
2. Place the basket into the Ninja Foodi.
3. Sprinkle the chili powder over the top of the salmon and then add the butter and lemon juice around the filets.
4. Place the pressure cooker lid on top of the pot and close the pressure valve to the seal position. Set the pressure cooker function to high heat and set the timer for 3 minutes.
5. Once the cooking cycle is complete, release the pressure quickly by carefully opening the steamer valve. Enjoy while hot
- **Nutrition Info:** Calories: 564g, Carbohydrates: 3g, Protein: 52g, Fat: 39g, Sugar: 1g, Sodium: 85mg

56. Creamy Herb 'n Parm Salmon

Servings: 2
Cooking Time: 10 Minutes

Ingredients:
- 2 frozen salmon filets
- 1/2 cup water
- 1 1/2 tsp minced garlic
- 1/4 cup heavy cream
- 1 cup parmesan cheese grated
- 1 tbsp chopped fresh chives
- 1 tbsp chopped fresh parsley
- 1 tbsp fresh dill
- 1 tsp fresh lemon juice
- Salt and pepper to taste

Directions:
1. Add water and trivet in pot. Place fillets on top of trivet.
2. Install pressure lid. Close Ninja Foodi, press pressure button, choose high settings, and set time to 4 minutes.
3. Once done cooking, do a quick release.
4. Transfer salmon to a serving plate. And remove trivet.
5. Press stop and then press sauté button on Ninja Foodi. Stir in heavy cream once water begins to boil. Boil for 3 minutes. Press stop and then stir in lemon juice, parmesan cheese, dill, parsley, and chives. Season with pepper and salt to taste. Pour over salmon.
6. Serve and enjoy.
- **Nutrition Info:** Calories: 423; carbohydrates: 6.4g; protein: 43.1g; fat: 25.0g

57. Tilapia Filet Topped With Mango-salsa

Servings: 2
Cooking Time: 5 Minutes

Ingredients:

- 1 cup coconut milk
- 1/2 to 1 tablespoon Thai green curry paste
- 1 tablespoon fish sauce
- Zest of 1 lime and juice of 1/2 lime
- 2 teaspoons sear button sugar
- 1 teaspoon garlic, minced
- 1 tablespoon fresh ginger, minced
- 2 6-oz Tilapia filet
- 1 lime, cut in thin slices
- A sprinkle of cilantro leaves and chopped scallion
- Mango salsa ingredients:
- 1 mango, peeled, seeded, and diced (about 3/4 cup small dice)
- 1 fresno or jalapeno chiles, minced
- 1 scallion, finely chopped
- A handful of cilantro leaves, chopped
- Juice of 1 lime

Directions:

1. In a bowl, mix well coconut milk, Thai green curry paste, fish sauce, lime juice, lime zest, sear button sugar, garlic, and ginger. Add fish and marinate for at least an hour.
2. Meanwhile, make the mango salsa by combining all ingredients in a separate bowl. Keep in the fridge.
3. Cut two 11x11-inch foil. Place one fish fillet in each foil. Top each equally with lime, scallion and cilantro. Seal foil packets.
4. Add a cup of water in Ninja Foodi, place trivet, and add foil packets on trivet.
5. Install pressure lid. Close Ninja Foodi, press pressure button, choose high settings, and set time to 5 minutes.
6. Once done cooking, do a quick release. Serve and enjoy with mango salsa on top.
- **Nutrition Info:** Calories: 372; carbohydrates: 28.5g; protein: 29.3g; fat: 15.6g

58. Mexican Swordfish

Servings: 4 Servings
Cooking Time: 8 Minutes

Ingredients:
- 4 Swordfish Steaks
- ½ cup water
- 1 cup chopped tomatoes
- ½ cup chopped onion
- 1 tbsp lime juice
- 1 jalapeno, seeds removed, chopped
- ½ tsp salt
- ¼ tsp ground black pepper

Directions:
1. Place the swordfish in the Ninja Foodi pot and add all the ingredients to the bowl.
2. Close the pressure seal lid and set the steamer valve to seal.
3. Cook on high pressure for 8 minutes then do a quick pressure release. Serve the swordfish while hot.
- **Nutrition Info:** Calories: 177g, Carbohydrates: 8g, Protein: 23g, Fat: 6g, Sugar: 5g, Sodium: 684

59. Stewed Mixed Seafood

Servings: 2
Cooking Time: 35 Minutes

Ingredients:
- 1 tbsp vegetable oil
- ½ 14.5-oz can fire-roasted tomatoes
- 1/2 cup diced onion
- 1/2 cup chopped carrots, or 1 cup chopped bell pepper
- 1/2 cup water
- 1/2 cup white wine or broth
- 1 bay leaf
- 1/2 tablespoon tomato paste
- 1 tablespoon minced garlic
- 1 teaspoon fennel seeds toasted and ground
- 1/2 teaspoon dried oregano
- 1 teaspoon salt
- 1 teaspoon red pepper flakes
- 2 cups mixed seafood such as fish chunks, shrimp, bay scallops, mussels and calamari rings, defrosted
- 1 tablespoon fresh lemon juice

Directions:
1. Press sauté button on Ninja Foodi and heat oil. Once hot, stir in onion and garlic. Sauté for 5 minutes. Stir in tomatoes, bay leaves, tomato paste, oregano, salt, and pepper flakes. Cook for 5 minutes. Press stop.
2. Stir in bell pepper, water, wine, and fennel seeds. Mix well.
3. Install pressure lid. Close Ninja Foodi, press pressure button, choose high settings, and set time to 15 minutes.
4. Once done cooking, do a quick release.
5. Stir in defrosted mixed seafood. Cover and let it cook for 10 minutes in residual heat.
6. Serve and enjoy with a dash of lemon juice.
- **Nutrition Info:** Calories: 202; carbohydrates: 10.0g; protein: 18.0g; fat: 10.0g

60. Pasta 'n Tuna Bake

Servings: 2
Cooking Time: 10 Minutes

Ingredients:
- 1 can cream-of-mushroom soup
- 1 1/2 cups water
- 1 1/4 cups macaroni pasta
- 1 can tuna
- 1/2 cup frozen peas
- 1/2 tsp salt
- 1 tsp pepper
- 1/2 cup shredded cheddar cheese

Directions:
1. Mix soup and water in Ninja Foodi.
2. Add remaining ingredients except for cheese. Stir.
3. Install pressure lid.
4. Close Ninja Foodi, press pressure button, choose high settings, and set time to 4 minutes.
5. Once done cooking, do a quick release.
6. Remove pressure lid.
7. Stir in cheese and roast for 5 minutes.
8. Serve and enjoy.
- **Nutrition Info:** Calories: 378; carbohydrates: 34.0g; protein: 28.0g; fat: 14.1g

61. Miso Glazed Salmon

Servings: 4
Cooking Time: 9 Minutes

Ingredients:
- 4 (4-oz.) (1-inch thick) frozen skinless salmon fillets
- Salt, to taste
- 2 tbsp. butter, softened
- 2 tbsp. red miso paste
- 2 heads baby bok choy, stems on, cut in half

Directions:
1. In the pot of Ninja Foodi, place ½ C. of water. In the pot, arrange the reversible rack in higher position. Season the salmon fillets with salt evenly.
2. Place the salmon fillets over the rack. Cover the Ninja Foodi with the pressure lid and place the pressure valve to "Seal" position.
3. Select "Pressure" and set to "High" for about 2 minutes.
4. Press "Start/Stop" to begin. Switch the valve to "Vent" and do a "Quick" release.
5. Meanwhile, spray the bok choy with cooking spray evenly.
6. In a bowl, add the butter and miso paste and mix well. Once all the pressure is released, open the lid. With paper towels, pat dry the salmon fillets and then, coat them with butter mixture evenly.
7. Arrange the bok choy around the salmon fillets,
8. Now, close the Ninja Foodi with crisping lid and select "Broil".
9. Set time to 7 minutes and select "Start/Stop" to begin.
10. Open the lid and serve the salmon fillets alongside the bok choy.
- **Nutrition Info:** Calories: 210; Carbohydrates: 9g; Protein: 24.2g; Fat: 9g; Sugar: 5.5g; Sodium: 897mg; Fiber: 3.4g

62. Fancy "rich" Guy Smoked Lobster

Servings: 4
Cooking Time: 35 Minutes

Ingredients:
- 6 Lobster Tails
- 4 garlic cloves
- ¼ c. butter

Directions:
1. Preheat the Ninja Foodi to 400 degrees F at first
2. Open the lobster tails gently by using kitchen scissors
3. Remove the lobster meat gently from the shells but keep it inside the shells
4. Take a plate and place it
5. Add some butter in a pan and allow it melt
6. Put some garlic cloves in it and heat it over medium-low heat
7. Pour the garlic butter mixture all over the lobster tail meat
8. Let the fryer to broil the lobster at 130 degrees F
9. Remove the lobster meat from Ninja Foodi and set aside
10. Use a fork to pull out the lobster meat from the shells entirely
11. Pour some garlic butter over it if needed

- **Nutrition Info:** 160 calories, 1g fat, 3g carbs, 20g protein

63. Jambalaya

Servings: 4 Servings
Cooking Time: 10 Minutes

Ingredients:
- 1 pound shrimp, deveined, shells removed
- 2 cups chicken broth
- 2 cloves of garlic, chopped
- 2 bell peppers, chopped
- 1 white onion, chopped
- 4 tomatoes, chopped
- 1 tsp dried basil
- 1 tsp dried oregano
- ½ tsp tsp salt
- 1/8 tsp ground black pepper
- ¼ cup shredded cheddar cheese

Directions:
1. Place the shrimp in the Ninja Foodi pot and sprinkle with the oregano, salt, basil and ground black pepper.
2. Add the broth, garlic, tomato, bell pepper and onion to the pot and close the pressure cooker lid.
3. Cook on high pressure for 10 minutes. Do a quick steam release and remove the lid.
4. Add the cream cheese and heavy cream and stir to blend.
5. Sprinkle the cheese on top of the chili and put the air crisper top on. Use the broil function to brown the cheese for 2 minutes.
- **Nutrition Info:** Calories: 150g, Carbohydrates: 2g, Protein: 36g, Fat: 0g, Sugar: 2g, Sodium: 438mg

Soups & Stews

64. Chickpea And Potato Soup

Servings: 2
Cooking Time: 15 Minutes

Ingredients:
- 1 tablespoon olive oil
- ½ onion, chopped
- 3 cloves of garlic, minced
- ½ cup chopped tomato
- 1/8 teaspoon fennel space
- ½ teaspoon onion powder
- ¼ teaspoon garlic powder
- ½ teaspoon oregano
- ¼ teaspoon cinnamon
- ½ teaspoon thyme
- 1 large potato, peeled and cubed
- ¾ cup carrots, chopped
- 1 ½ cups cooked chickpeas
- 1 cup water
- 1 cup almond milk
- 1 cup kale, chopped
- Salt and pepper to taste

Directions:
1. Press the sauté button on the Ninja Foodi and sauté the onion and garlic until fragrant.
2. Stir in the tomatoes, fennel, onion powder, garlic powder, oregano, cinnamon, and thyme. Stir until well-combined.
3. Add the rest of the ingredients. Install pressure lid. Close Ninja Foodi, press the pressure button, choose high settings, and set time to 10 minutes.
4. Once done cooking, do a quick release. Serve and enjoy.
- **Nutrition Info:** Calories: 543; carbohydrates: 91.0g; protein: 17.7g; fat: 12g

65. White Chicken Chili

Servings: 6-8 Servings
Cooking Time: 40-50 Minutes

Ingredients:
- 4 cups chicken, cooked and chopped
- 3 ½ cups chicken broth
- 2 cans white beans, drained and rinsed
- 2 cans green chilies, diced
- 1 onion, chopped
- 2 teaspoons olive oil
- 2 teaspoons cumin
- 2 teaspoons oregano
- 1 clove garlic, chopped fine
- 1 teaspoon cayenne pepper

Directions:
1. Set cooker to sauté on med-high heat and add oil. Once oil is hot, add onion and cook 3-4 minutes or they are translucent. Add garlic and cook another minute. Add green chilies and spices and cook 2 more minutes, stirring frequently.
2. Add broth and beans. Secure lid. Set to pressure cooking function with low pressure. Set timer for 20 minutes. When timer goes off, use quick release to remove the lid.
3. Set back to sauté on low heat. Add chicken and cook 10-15 minutes, stirring occasionally. Serve garnished as desired.

66. Verde Pork Stew

Servings: 6 Servings
Cooking Time: 4 – 8 Hours

Ingredients:
- 1 – 1 ½ pound pork tenderloin
- 2 cups chicken broth
- 1 16-ounce jar salsa verde
- 1 15-ounce can black beans, rinsed and drained
- 1 teaspoon cumin

Directions:
1. Place all ingredients in the cooking pot. Set to slow cooker functions. Cook 3-4 hours on high heat, or 6-8 hours on low.
2. When pork is tender, transfer it to a bowl and shred with two forks. Return it to the pot and stir to combine. Serve garnished as desired.

67. Creamy Chicken & Mushroom Soup

Servings: 6 Servings
Cooking Time: 15 Minutes

Ingredients:

- 6 chicken thighs, boneless, skinless and cut into 1-inch pieces
- 4 cups chicken broth
- 1 cup cremini mushrooms, sliced thin
- 3 carrots, peeled and chopped fine
- 2 stalks celery, chopped fine
- 1 onion, chopped fine
- ½ cup half-and-half
- ¼ cup flour
- 3 cloves garlic, chopped fine
- 2 tablespoons butter
- 2 tablespoons fresh parsley, chopped
- 1 tablespoon olive oil
- ½ teaspoon thyme
- 1 sprig rosemary
- 1 bay leaf
- Salt & pepper

Directions:

1. Add the olive oil to the pot and set to sauté on medium heat. Sprinkle the chicken with salt and pepper and add to the pot. Cook till brown, about 2-3 minutes, set aside.
2. Add the butter and let it melt. Once melted, add the vegetables and cook till tender, about 3-4 minutes. Stir in thyme and cook 1 minute more.
3. Stir in flour till lightly browned, about 1 minute. Add the broth, bay leaf, rosemary and chicken and cook, stirring constantly, till soup thickens, about 4-5 minutes.
4. Stir in the half-and-half and continue cooking till heated through, 1-2 minutes. Discard bay leaf and rosemary sprig. Serve immediately.

68. Spiced Potato-cauliflower Chowder

Servings: 2
Cooking Time: 7 Minutes

Ingredients:
- 1 head cauliflower, cut into florets
- 2 small red potatoes, peeled and sliced
- 4 cups vegetable stock
- 6 cloves of garlic, minced
- 1 onion, diced
- 1 cup heavy cream
- 2 bay leaves
- Salt and pepper to taste
- 2 stalks of green onions

Directions:
1. Place the cauliflower, potatoes, vegetable stock, garlic, onion, heavy cream, and bay leaves in the Ninja Foodi. Season with salt and pepper to taste.
2. Install pressure lid. Close Ninja Foodi, press the pressure button, choose high settings, and set time to 6 minutes.
3. Once done cooking, do a quick release.
4. Open the lid and stir in the green onions.
5. Serve and enjoy.
- **Nutrition Info:** Calories: 448; carbohydrates: 47.7g; protein: 10.1g; fat: 24.1g

69. Seafood Stew

Servings: 4 Servings
Cooking Time: 25 Mins

Ingredients:
- 1 pound mixed lobster, shrimp and cod
- 3 ½ cups water
- 3 ½ cups tomatoes, crushed
- 2 cups potatoes, cubed
- 1 ½ cups celery, sliced
- 1 ½ cups onions, chopped
- 1 ½ cups carrots, sliced
- ¼ cups shallots, chopped
- 4 - 6 cloves of garlic, chopped fine
- 1 teaspoon salt
- 1 teaspoon pepper
- 1 teaspoon basil
- 1 teaspoon Greek seasoning
- 1 teaspoon Sriracha sauce

Directions:
1. Place all the vegetables, except the potatoes into the cooking pot. Add tomatoes, water and seasonings. Secure lid and set to pressure cooking on high. Set timer for 10 minutes.
2. When timer goes off, use quick release to remove the lid. Add the potatoes and pressure cook another 8 minutes. Use quick release again.
3. Set to sauté on medium heat. Stir in the seafood and cook till shrimp and lobster is pink and the stew is heated through, about 5 minutes. Serve.

70. Greens & Beans Soup

Servings: 8 – 10 Servings
Cooking Time: 6 Hours

Ingredients:

- 1 pound bean soup mix, rinsed and debris removed
- 6 cups chicken broth
- 6 cups mustard or collard greens, chopped
- 2 smoked turkey wings.
- 2 cups baby Portabella mushrooms
- 1 onion, chopped
- 1 can tomatoes, diced
- 1 cup carrots, cut into chunks
- 7 cloves garlic, chopped fine
- ¾ cup red wine
- 2 tablespoons Italian seasoning
- 1 teaspoon sage
- 2 bay leaves
- Salt & pepper

Directions:

1. Add all of the ingredients, but use only half the greens, to the cooking pot. Secure lid and select slow cooking on high. Cook 5 ½ hours.
2. Remove turkey wings. When cool enough to handle, remove any meat from the bones and add it back to the soup. Add remaining greens and cook another 15 minutes. Serve topped with Parmesan cheese if desired.

71. Sweet Potato 'n Garbanzo Soup

Servings: 2
Cooking Time: 10 Minutes

Ingredients:
- 1/2 yellow onion, chopped
- 1/2 tablespoon garlic, minced
- 1 can garbanzo beans, drained
- 1/2-pound sweet potatoes, peeled and chopped
- Salt and pepper to taste
- 1/2 teaspoon ground ginger
- 1/2 teaspoon ground cumin
- 1/2 teaspoon ground coriander
- 1/2 teaspoon ground cinnamon
- 2 cups vegetable broth
- 2 cups spinach, torn

Directions:
1. Place all ingredients in the Ninja Foodi except for the spinach.
2. Install pressure lid. Close Ninja Foodi, press the manual button, choose high settings, and set time to 10 minutes.
3. Once done cooking, do a quick release.
4. Open the lid and stir in the spinach. Press the sauté button and allow to simmer until the spinach wilts.
5. Serve and enjoy.
- **Nutrition Info:** Calories: 165; carbohydrates: 32.3g; protein: 6.3g; fat: 1.1g

72. Autumn Stew

Servings: 4 -6 Servings
Cooking Time: 8 Hours

Ingredients:
- 1 pound smoked sausage, sliced, not too thin
- 4 potatoes, peeled and quartered
- 3 carrots, peeled and chopped
- 3 stalks celery, sliced
- 2-3 turnips, peeled and cubed
- 1 small cabbage, cut into chunks
- 1 large can of tomatoes, diced
- 1 teaspoon sage
- 1 teaspoon oregano
- 1 teaspoon basil
- ½ teaspoon thyme
- ½ teaspoon rosemary
- Salt & pepper

Directions:
1. Layer the ingredients in the cooking pot; carrots, turnips, celery, potatoes and cabbage, sprinkling each layer with a little of the herbs, salt and pepper.
2. Spread tomatoes, with liquid, over cabbage and top with sausage. Sprinkle more seasonings on top.
3. Secure the lid and select slow cooking function. The stew will take 7-8 hours on low or 4-5 on high heat. The stew is done with vegetables are tender. Stir well before serving.

73. Sunchoke & Asparagus Soup

Servings: 4 Servings
Cooking Time: 15 Minutes

Ingredients:
- 1 pound asparagus, cut off 1 ½ inches of the tips, discard woody ends and chop remaining into 1-inch pieces
- 3 cups vegetable broth
- ½ pound sunchokes, peeled and chopped
- 1 ½ cups potato, peeled and chopped
- 2 large shallots, peeled and sliced
- 2 tablespoons olive oil
- ½ teaspoons salt
- 1/8 teaspoon white pepper

Directions:
1. Add oil to the pot and set to sauté on medium heat. Add shallot and cook till soft. Add the vegetables along with the broth. Secure the lid and set to pressure cooking on high. Set the timer for 10 minutes. When the timer goes off, use quick release to remove the lid.
2. While the vegetables are cooking, bring a small pot of water to a boil and prepare an ice bath in a bowl. Add the asparagus tips to the boiling water and cook 2 minutes. Transfer the tips to the ice bath with a slotted spoon.
3. Once the vegetables in the cooking pot are tender, use an immersion blender to puree till smooth. Season with salt and pepper to taste.
4. To serve, ladle soup into bowls, divide the asparagus tips among them and drizzle a little olive oil over the top.

74. Sweet Potato & Black Bean Stew

Servings: 6 Servings
Cooking Time: 25 Minutes

Ingredients:
- 4 cups vegetable broth
- 4 cups kale, chopped
- 3 cups sweet potatoes, peeled and cubed
- 1 can black beans, rinsed and drained
- 1 large onion, chopped
- 4 cloves garlic, chopped fine
- 3 green onions, sliced thin
- 2 radishes, sliced thin
- 2 tablespoons olive oil
- 1 tablespoon lime juice
- 2 teaspoons oregano
- 1 ½ teaspoons cumin
- 1 teaspoon garlic powder
- ½. teaspoon black pepper
- ½ teaspoon salt
- ¼ teaspoon cayenne

Directions:
1. Add the oil to the pot and set to sauté on med-high heat. Add the onions and cook till translucent, about 3 minutes. Reduce heat to medium, add the garlic and seasonings and cook for 30 seconds.
2. Add the potatoes, broth, beans and salt and bring to a low boil. Cook 15 minutes, or till potatoes are tender.
3. Turn off the heat and stir in kale, green onions and lime juice. Serve.

75. Beefy White Cream Soup

Servings: 2
Cooking Time: 17 Minutes

Ingredients:
- ½ pounds stew meat
- 2 cups beef broth
- 1 1/2 tablespoons Worcestershire sauce
- ½ teaspoon Italian seasoning
- 1 teaspoon onion powder
- 1 teaspoons garlic powder
- 1/4 cup sour cream
- 3 ounces mushrooms, sliced
- Salt and pepper to taste
- 2 ounces short noodles, blanched

Directions:
1. Place the meat, broth, Worcestershire sauce, Italian seasoning, onion powder, garlic powder, sour cream, and mushrooms. Season with salt and pepper to taste.
2. Install pressure lid. Close Ninja Foodi, press the pressure button, choose high settings, and set time to 12 minutes.
3. Once done cooking, do a quick release. Open the lid and press the sauté button. Stir in the noodles and allow to simmer for 5 minutes.
4. Serve and enjoy.
- **Nutrition Info:** Calories: 599 ; carbohydrates: 65g; protein: 39.6g; fat: 20.1g

76. Lamb Provencal

Servings: 4 Servings
Cooking Time: 40 Minutes

Ingredients:

- 1 pound lamb stew meat
- 4 cups beef broth
- 2 cups mushrooms, quartered
- 2 cups sweet potatoes, peeled and cubed
- 2 cups turnips, peeled and cubed
- 1 cup dry red wine
- 1 shallot, chopped fine
- ¾ cup flour
- 2 tablespoons olive oil
- 1 tablespoon Herbes de Provence
- 2 bay leaves
- 1 sprig rosemary
- 1 teaspoon garlic, chopped fine
- ½ teaspoon salt
- a few grinds of pepper

Directions:

1. In a large bowl, mix together flour with some salt and pepper. Add the lamb and toss to coat well.
2. Add the oil to the cooking pot and set to sauté on med-high heat. When hot, add the lamb, shallot and garlic and cook till lamb begins to brown.
3. Add the broth, wine and seasonings and stir to combine. Secure the lid and set to pressure cooking on high. Set the timer for 30 minutes.
4. When the timer goes off, use quick release to remove the lid. Add the vegetables and secure the lid again. Cook on high pressure for 10 minutes.
5. Use quick release to remove the lid. Stir well and serve.

77. Duck Ale Chili

Servings: 6 Servings
Cooking Time: 45 Minutes

Ingredients:
- 1 ½ pound duck breast
- 1 large can fire roasted tomatoes, diced
- 1 can kidney beans, rinsed and drained
- 1 can great northern beans, rinsed and drained
- 1 bottle brown ale
- 1 small can tomato paste
- 1 cup white onion, chopped fine
- 5 cloves garlic, chopped fine
- 2 tablespoons chili powder
- 1 tablespoon Worcestershire
- 1 tablespoon oregano
- 2 teaspoons cumin
- 1 teaspoon salt
- 1 teaspoon ground black pepper
- 1 teaspoon smoked paprika
- 1 teaspoon onion powder
- 1 teaspoon red pepper flakes
- ½ teaspoon cayenne pepper
- Garnishes:
- 1 cup mozzarella cheese, grated
- ½ cup chopped cilantro

Directions:
1. Score the fat on the duck and sprinkle with salt. Place, fat side down, in the cooking pot.
2. Select sauté on medium heat and sear the duck till golden brown and most of the fat has been rendered. Transfer duck to a plate.
3. Add the onions and cook till they soften, about 5 minutes. Add the duck back to the pot along with remaining ingredients.
4. Secure the lid and set to pressure cooking on high. Set the timer for 30 minutes. When the timer goes off, use manual release to remove the lid.
5. Remove the duck and shred with two forks. Return it to the pot and stir well.
6. Ladle into bowl and top with garnishes before serving.

78. Vegan Approver Tortilla Soup

Servings: 2
Cooking Time: 40 Minutes

Ingredients:

- 1/2 cup diced onion
- 1/2 bell pepper, diced
- 1/2 jalapeno pepper, diced
- 1 1/4 cups vegetable broth
- 1/2 can tomato sauce
- 1/4 cup salsa verde
- 1/2 tablespoon tomato paste
- 1/2 can black beans, drained and rinsed
- 1/2 can pinto beans, drained and rinsed
- 1/2 cup fresh corn kernels
- ½ teaspoon chili powder
- ½ teaspoon garlic powder
- Salt and pepper to taste
- 2 tbsp heavy cream

Directions:

1. Place all ingredients in the Ninja Foodi except for the heavy cream and give a good stir.
2. Install pressure lid. Close Ninja Foodi, press the manual button, choose high settings, and set time to 20 minutes.
3. Once done cooking, do a quick release.
4. Open the lid and press the sauté button. Stir in the heavy cream and allow to simmer for 5 minutes.
5. Serve and enjoy.

- **Nutrition Info:** Calories: 341; carbohydrates: 48.7g; protein: 8.6g; fat: 12.4g

79. Cheesy Onion Soup

Servings: 4 Servings
Cooking Time: 10 Minutes

Ingredients:

- 2 ¼ cups sharp cheddar cheese, grated
- 1 Vidalia onion, sliced thin
- 1 can chicken broth
- 1 cup milk
- ¼ cup celery, chopped fine
- ¼ cup dry white wine
- 2 tablespoons butter
- 2 tablespoons flour
- 1 tablespoon chives, chopped
- ½ teaspoon pepper
- ½ teaspoon dry mustard

Directions:

1. Add butter to the cooking pot and set to sauté on medium heat. Once melted, add onion and celery and cook 3 minutes, stirring often.
2. Stir in flour, pepper and mustard. Slowly stir in the milk, broth and wine. Bring to a boil and cook, stirring, one minute.
3. Stir in the cheese, reduce heat to low and while stirring constantly, cook till cheese is melted. Ladle into bowls and garnish with chopped chives.

80. Deliciously Traditional Clam Chowder

Servings: 2
Cooking Time: 17 Minutes

Ingredients:

- 2 6.5-oz cans chopped clams (reserve the clam juice)
- Water
- 2 slices bacon, chopped
- 1 1/2 tbsp butter
- 1 onion, diced
- 1 stalks celery, diced
- 1 sprig fresh thyme
- 1 cloves garlic, pressed or finely minced
- 1/2 tsp kosher salt or more
- 1/4 tsp pepper
- ½-lb potatoes, diced
- 1/2 tsp sugar
- 1/2 cup half and half
- Chopped chives, for garnish

Directions:

1. Drain the clam juice into a 2-cup measuring cup. Add enough water to make 2 cups of liquid. Set the clams and juice/water aside.
2. Press sauté button and cook bacon for 3 minutes until fat has rendered out of it, but not crispy. Add the butter, onion, celery, and thyme. Cook for 5 minutes while frequently stirring. Add the garlic, salt, and pepper. Cook for 1 minute, stirring frequently.
3. Add the potatoes, sugar (if using) and clam juice/water mixture and deglaze pot. Press stop.
4. Close Ninja Foodi, press pressure cook button, choose high settings, and set time to 4 minutes. Once done cooking, do a natural release for 3 minutes and then do a quick release. Mash the potatoes. Stir in half and half and the clams. Mix well.
5. Serve and enjoy garnished with chives.
- **Nutrition Info:** Calories: 381; carbohydrates: 32.8g; protein: 29.3g; fat: 14.7

81. Sausage & Spinach Stew

Servings: 4 Servings
Cooking Time: 20 Minutes

Ingredients:
- 12 ounce Italian chicken sausage, fully cooked
- 4 cups chicken broth
- 1 bag spinach
- 1 can cannellini beans, rinsed and drained
- 1 cup ditalini pasta
- ½ cup dry white wine
- 4 cloves garlic, chopped
- 1 tablespoon olive oil
- Pepper
- Parmesan cheese

Directions:
1. Add oil to cooker and set to sauté on medium heat. Add the sausage and cook, stirring often, till brown, about 4-5 minutes. Remove to a plate.
2. Add the garlic and cook, stirring, 1 minute. Add the wine and simmer to deglaze the pan, about 1 minutes.
3. Add the broth and pasta and bring to a boil. Cook till pasta is tender, about 8-10 minutes. Stir in the beans, sausage and pepper and cook till heated through. Turn the cooker off and stir in the spinach. Ladle into bowls and top with Parmesan cheese before serving.

82. Healthy Celery 'n Kale Soup

Servings: 2
Cooking Time: 35 Minutes

Ingredients:

- 1 teaspoon olive oil
- 1/2 onion, diced
- 1 clove garlic, minced
- 1 stalk celery, chopped
- 1 carrot, peeled and chopped
- 1 small potato, peeled and diced
- 1 teaspoon herbs de provence
- 1/2 can diced tomatoes
- 2 cups vegetable broth
- 2 cups green lentils, soaked overnight
- Salt and pepper to taste
- 1 cup kale, torn

Directions:

1. Press the sauté button on the Ninja Foodi and heat the oil.
2. Sauté the onion, garlic, and celery until fragrant.
3. Stir in the carrots, potatoes, herbs, tomatoes, vegetable broth and lentils. Season with salt and pepper to taste.
4. Install pressure lid. Close Ninja Foodi, press the pressure button, choose high settings, and set time to 30 minutes.
5. Once done cooking, do a quick release. Open the lid and stir in the kale while still hot. Serve and enjoy.
- **Nutrition Info:** Calories: 331; carbohydrates: 53g; protein: 23g; fat: 3g

83. Chili-quinoa 'n Black Bean Soup

Servings: 2
Cooking Time: 20 Minutes

Ingredients:
- 1/2 bell pepper, diced
- 1 medium-sized sweet potatoes, peeled and diced
- 1/2 onion, diced
- 1 clove garlic, minced
- 1 stalk celery, chopped
- 1 1/3 cups vegetable broth
- 1 tablespoon tomato paste
- 1/3 cup diced tomatoes
- 1/3 can black beans, rinsed and drained
- 1 teaspoon each of paprika and cumin
- Salt to taste
- 2 tbsp quinoa
- 2 cups vegetable broth

Directions:
1. Place all ingredients in the Ninja Foodi. Give a good stir.
2. Install pressure lid.
3. Close Ninja Foodi, press the pressure button, choose high settings, and set time to 20 minutes.
4. Once done cooking, do a quick release.
5. Serve and enjoy.
- **Nutrition Info:** Calories: 377; carbohydrates: 73.7g; protein: 18.1g; fat: 1.0g

84. Shrimp & Mango Curry

Servings: 4 Servings
Cooking Time: 15 Minutes

Ingredients:
- 1 ¼ pounds shrimp, peeled and deveined
- 2 cups clam juice
- 1 can coconut milk
- 3 mangoes, chopped
- 1 onion, chopped
- 2 stalks celery, sliced
- 1 bunch scallions, sliced
- 4 cloves garlic, chopped fine
- 1 serrano chili, seeded and chopped fine
- 2 tablespoons curry powder
- 1 tablespoon olive oil
- 1 teaspoon thyme
- ¼ teaspoon salt

Directions:
1. Add oil to cooker and set to sauté on medium heat. Add onion and celery and cook, stirring often, till the onion begins to brown, about 3-5 minutes.
2. Add garlic, chili, curry powder and thyme, stir constantly and cook 30 seconds. Add the clam juice, coconut milk and mangoes and increase the heat to med-high. Bring to a simmer and cook, stirring often, for 5 minutes.
3. Add 3 cups of the soup to a blender and process till smooth. Return it to the pot and bring back to simmer. Add shrimp and cook till they turn pink, about 3 minutes. Stir in scallions and salt and serve.

Dessert Recipes

85. Key Lime Curd

Servings: 6 Servings
Cooking Time: 10 Minutes

Ingredients:
- 3 oz butter
- ½ cup baking stevia
- 2 eggs
- 2 egg yolks
- 2/3 cup key lime juice
- 2 tsp lime zest

Directions:
1. Blend the butter and stevia then add in the eggs slowly, creating an emulsion.
2. Add the key lime juice and zest and the separate into mason jars
3. Add 1 ½ cups of water to the bottom of the Ninja Foodi and place the mason jars on top of the metal trivet inside the pot.
4. Place the pressure cooker lid on the pot and set the pressure cooker function to high pressure for 10 minutes. Let the pressure release naturally after the cooking time is completed.
5. Let cool and then enjoy.
- **Nutrition Info:** Calories: 151g, Carbohydrates: 3g, Protein: 3g, Fat: 15g, Sugar: 1g, Sodium: 109mg

86. Nutty Cinnamon 'n Cranberry Cake

Servings: 2
Cooking Time: 25 Minutes

Ingredients:

- 2 tbsp cashew milk (or use any dairy or non-dairy milk you prefer)
- 1 medium egg
- 1/2 tsp vanilla extract
- 1/2 cup almond flour
- 2 tbsp monk fruit (or use your preferred sweetener)
- 1/4 tsp baking powder
- 1/4 tsp cinnamon
- 1/8 tsp salt
- 3 tbsp fresh cranberries
- 2 tbsp cup chopped pecans

Directions:

1. In blender, add all wet ingredients: and mix well. Add all dry ingredients: except for cranberries and pecans. Blend well until smooth.
2. Lightly grease baking pot of Ninja Foodi with cooking spray. Pour in batter. Drizzle cranberries on top and then followed by pecans.
3. For 20 minutes, cook on 330 ºF.
4. Let stand for 5 minutes.
5. Serve and enjoy.

- **Nutrition Info:** Calories: 98; carbs: 11.7g; protein: 1.7g; fat: 4.9g

87. Almond Cheese Cake

Servings: 6 Servings
Cooking Time: 20 Minutes

Ingredients:
- Crust: ½ cup almond flour
- 2 Tbsp stevia
- 2 Tbsp melted butter
- Filling: 16 oz cream cheese
- ½ cup baking stevia
- 1 egg
- 2 egg yolks
- ¼ cup sour cream
- ¾ cup heavy cream
- 1 tsp almond extract

Directions:
1. In a small bowl, mix all the ingredients for the crust together. Press the crust into a 7" spring form pan wrapped in foil. Set aside
2. Add the cream cheese, stevia and cocoa powder to a food processor and blend. Add the egg and yolks and blend again. Add remaining ingredients and mix just to combine. Pour cheesecake mix on top of the prepared crust.
3. Place the pan in the Ninja Foodi bowl on top of the metal trivet. Add 2 cups of water to the bowl under the cake. Place the pressure cooker lid on and set it to high pressure for 20 minutes. Allow the pot to naturally release the pressure once he cooking time is done. Chill and then serve.
- **Nutrition Info:** Calories: 474g, Carbohydrates: 10g, Protein:8g, Fat: 46g, Sugar: 4g, Sodium: 338g

88. Caramel Apple Chimichangas

Servings: 1 Dozen
Cooking Time: 6 Mins

Ingredients:
- 12 10-inch flour tortillas
- 7 Granny Smith apples, peeled, cored and sliced
- 1 lemon, juice and zest
- ¾ cup light brown sugar
- ¼ cup flour
- ¾ teaspoon ground cinnamon
- Cinnamon sugar
- Caramel sauce

Directions:
1. Preheat air fryer to 400 degrees.
2. Mix the brown sugar, flour and cinnamon together in small bowl.
3. In a large bowl, toss the apples with the lemon juice, then stir in the sugar mixture making sure to coat all of the apples.
4. Warm the tortillas so they are soft enough to fold. Place ½ - ¾ cup apples in the center of tortilla and fold like a burrito. You can seal the edge with water or use toothpicks.
5. Lightly spray the outsides with cooking spray and sprinkle with the cinnamon sugar.
6. Cook them in batches in the fryer, 6-7 minutes, turning halfway through.
7. Drizzle with the caramel sauce, or serve them with the caramel sauce for dipping.

89. Crème Brûlée

Servings: 4
Cooking Time: 25 Minutes

Ingredients:

- 1 c. heavy cream
- ½ tbsp. vanilla extract
- 3 egg yolks
- 1 pinch salt
- ¼ c. stevia

Directions:

1. Mix together egg yolks, vanilla extract, heavy cream and salt in a bowl and beat until combined.
2. Divide the mixture into 4 greased ramekins evenly and transfer the ramekins in the basket of Ninja Foodi.
3. Press "Bake/Roast" and set the timer for about 15 minutes at 365 degrees F.
4. Remove from the Ninja Foodi and cover the ramekins with a plastic wrap.
5. Refrigerate to chill for about 3 hours and serve chilled.
- **Nutrition Info:** 149 calories, 14.5g fat, 1.6g carbs, 2.6g protein

90. Vanilla Yogurt

Servings: 2
Cooking Time: 3 Hours 20 Minutes

Ingredients:
- ½ c. full-fat milk
- ¼ c. yogurt starter
- 1 c. heavy cream
- ½ tbsp. pure vanilla extract
- 2 scoops stevia

Directions:
1. Pour milk in the pot of Ninja Foodi and stir in heavy cream, vanilla extract and stevia.
2. Allow the yogurt to sit and press "Slow Cooker" and cook on Low for about 3 hours.
3. Add the yogurt starter in 1 cup of milk and return this mixture to the pot.
4. Lock the lid and wrap the Ninja Foodi in two small towels.
5. Let sit for about 9 hours and allow the yogurt to culture.
6. Dish out in a serving bowl or refrigerate to serve.
- **Nutrition Info:** 292 calories, 26.2g fat, 8.2g carbs, 5.2g protein

91. Scrumptiously Molten Lava Cake

Servings: 3
Cooking Time: 6 Minutes

Ingredients:
- 1 egg
- 4 tablespoon sugar
- 2 tablespoon olive oil
- 4 tablespoon milk
- 4 tablespoon all-purpose flour
- 1 tablespoon cacao powder
- ½ teaspoon baking powder
- Pinch of salt
- Powdered sugar for dusting

Directions:
1. Grease two ramekins with butter or oil. Set aside
2. Pour 1 cup of water in the Ninja Foodi and place the steamer rack.
3. In a medium bowl, mix all the ingredients except the powdered sugar. Blend until well combined.
4. Pour in the ramekins. Place the ramekins in the Ninja Foodi.
5. Install pressure lid and close. Press the pressure button and cook on high for 6 minutes.
6. Once the Ninja Foodi beeps, remove the ramekin.
7. Sprinkle powdered sugar once cooled.
8. Serve and enjoy.
- **Nutrition Info:** Calories: 290; carbohydrates: 30.0g; protein: 5.2g; fat: 16.6g

92. Almond Cake

Servings: 8 Servings
Cooking Time: 25 Minutes

Ingredients:
- 8 Tbsp butter
- ½ cup Baking Stevia
- 1 egg
- 1 tsp vanilla
- 2 cups almond flour
- 2 tsp baking powder
- 1 tsp salt
- 1 cup chopped Almonds
- ½ cup buttermilk

Directions:
1. Use an electric mixer to cream the butter and stevia together until they are light and fluffy.
2. Mix the vanilla and eggs in a small bowl then add to the mixer with the butter blend until just combined.
3. Add the remaining dry ingredients to the mixer and fold together by hand. Add the buttermilk and mix until smooth.
4. Add the almonds to the batter and mix briefly.
5. Pour the cake batter into your Ninja Foodi and place the lid on.
6. Press the air crisp button and set the temperature to 350 degrees and program the timer to 25 minutes.
7. Once cooked, a toothpick should come out of the center of the cake cleanly. Allow to cool and serve.
- **Nutrition Info:** Calories: 295 g, Carbohydrates: 6g , Protein: 7g, Fat: 29 g, Sugar: 1g, Sodium: 165 mg

93. Individual S'mores Pies

Servings: 6 – 12 Pies
Cooking Time: 10 Minutes

Ingredients:
- 2 sheets of puff pastry, thawed
- 2 chocolate bars
- 1 cup mini marshmallows
- ½ cup graham cracker crumbs
- 1 egg, lightly beaten

Directions:
1. Roll out the pastry dough on a lightly floured surface. Cut into 2-3 inch squares, or the size you desire.
2. In the center of half the squares, place a piece of chocolate, some marshmallows and graham crumbs. Moisten the edges of the pastry with water and add the remaining squares on top. Press the edges together. Brush the tops with egg wash.
3. Place 2-3 pies in the air fryer basket at a time, add the Tender Crisp lid and set the temperature to 330 degrees. Bake 5-7 minutes or till the outside is puffed and golden brown. Cool slightly before serving. You can drizzle the tops with melted chocolate or melted marshmallow cream.

94. Fudge Divine

Servings: 24
Cooking Time: 6 Hours 20 Minutes

Ingredients:

- ½ tsp. organic vanilla extract
- 1 c. heavy whipping cream
- 2 oz. softened butter
- 2 oz. chopped 70% dark chocolate

Directions:

1. Press "Sauté" and "Md:Hi" on Ninja Foodi and add vanilla and heavy cream.
2. Sauté for about 5 minutes and select "Lo".
3. Sauté for about 10 minutes and add butter and chocolate.
4. Sauté for about 2 minutes and transfer this mixture in a serving dish.
5. Refrigerate it for few hours and serve chilled.
- **Nutrition Info:** 292 calories, 26.2g fat, 8.2g carbs, 5.2g protein

95. Excellent Strawberry Toast Pastries

Servings: 8
Cooking Time: 30 Minutes

Ingredients:
- 1 refrigerated pie crust, at room temperature
- ¼ c. simple strawberry jam
- Vanilla icing
- Rainbow sprinkles

Directions:
1. Place Cook and Crisp basket in the pot and close the crisping lead, pre-heat at 350 degrees F on Air Crisp mode for 5 minutes
2. Roll out pie crust on a lightly floured surface, shaping it into a large rectangle, cut dough into 8 rectangles
3. Spoon a tablespoon of jam to the center of each of 4 dough rectangles, leaving ½ inch border
4. Brush edges of filled dough with water, top each with the other 4 dough rectangles and gently press edges to seal
5. Place pastries in your pre-heated basket and coat with cooking spray
6. Arrange pastries in the Cook and Crisp basket in a single layer
7. Close crisping lid and Air Crisp for 10 minutes at 350 degrees F
8. Repeat until all pastries are done, frost pastries with vanilla icing and top with sprinkles
9. Enjoy!
- **Nutrition Info:** 363 calories, 15g fat, 55g carbs, 2g protein

96. Raspberry Mug Cake

Servings: 2 Servings
Cooking Time: 10 Minutes

Ingredients:
- 2/3 cup almond flour
- 2 eggs
- 2 Tbsp maple syrup
- 1 tsp vanilla
- 1/8 tsp salt
- 1 cup fresh raspberries

Directions:
1. Mix all the ingredients together except the raspberries. Fold well to ensure no lumps.
2. Fold in raspberries
3. Pour the batter into two 8 oz mason jars and cover the jars with foil.
4. Place the metal trivet into the Ninja Foodi and add 1 cup of water to the bowl.
5. Place the two mason jars on top of the trivet and close the pressure cooker top. Seal the steamer valve and set the timer to 10 minutes
6. Let the pressure naturally release and then open the lid and enjoy the warm cake.
- **Nutrition Info:** Calories: 215g, Carbohydrates: 10g, Protein: 9g, Fat: 10g, Sugar: 16g, Sodium: 82mg

97. Blackberry Brioche Bread Pudding

Servings: 4-6 Servings

Cooking Time: 30 – 46 Minutes

Ingredients:

- 4 cups brioche bread cubes, loosely packed
- ½ pint blackberries, rinse and pat dry
- 1 cup milk
- 2 eggs
- ½ cup sugar
- 1 teaspoon vanilla
- pinch of salt

Directions:

1. Lightly spray the cooking pot with cooking spray.
2. Place the bread cubes and berries in the pot.
3. In a mixing bowl, whisk remaining ingredients together and pour over the bread and berries.
4. Add the Tender Crisp lid and set to 350 degrees. Bake 45 minutes, or till the pudding puffs up and is starting to brown on top. Serve warm.

98. Banana Bundt Cake

Servings: 4 -6 Servings
Cooking Time: 30 Minutes

Ingredients:
- 1 cup flour
- 1 ripe banana, mashed
- 1/3 cup brown sugar, packed
- ¼ cup butter, soft
- 1 egg
- 2-3 tablespoons walnuts, chopped
- 2 tablespoons honey
- ½ teaspoon cinnamon
- Pinch of salt

Directions:
1. Preheat air fryer to 320 degrees. Lightly spray a small ring cake pan with cooking spray.
2. Place the butter and sugar in a mixing bowl and beat till creamy. Add egg, banana and honey and stir till smooth.
3. Add the dry ingredients and stir to mix well. Pour into prepared pan.
4. Add the rack to the bottom of the cooking pot and place pan on it. Add the Tender Crisp lid and bake 30 minutes or it passes the toothpick test.
5. Carefully remove the pan from the cooker and let cool 10 minutes before transferring to a serving plate. Garnish if desired.

99. Chocolatey 'n Peanut Butter Cakes

Servings: 2
Cooking Time: 15 Minutes

Ingredients:

- 1/2 can black beans, drained and rinsed
- 1/4 cup cocoa powder, unsweetened
- 1/4 cup egg whites
- 2 tbsp canned pumpkin
- 2 tbsp unsweetened applesauce
- 2 tbsp sear button sugar
- 1/2 teaspoon vanilla extract
- ¾ teaspoon baking powder
- ¼ teaspoon salt
- 1 1/2 tablespoon peanut butter baking chips

Directions:

1. Place all the ingredients except the peanut butter chips inside a food processor. Process until smooth.
2. Add the peanut butter chips and fold until evenly distributed within the batter.
3. Place the batter in a ramekin sprayed with cooking oil.
4. Place a steam rack in the Ninja Foodi and add 1 cup water.
5. Place the ramekins with the batter onto the steamer rack.
6. Install pressure lid. Close the lid and press the manual button. Cook on high for 10 minutes.
7. Do natural pressure release.
8. Serve chilled.
- **Nutrition Info:** Calories: 246; carbohydrates: 34.9g; protein: 12.0g; fat: 6.5g

100. Chocolate Cheese Cake(2)

Servings: 6
Cooking Time: 25 Minutes

Ingredients:
- 2 c. softened cream cheese
- 2 eggs
- 2 tbsps. cocoa powder
- 1 tsp. pure vanilla extract
- ½ c. swerve

Directions:
1. Place eggs, cocoa powder, vanilla extract, swerve and cream cheese in an immersion blender and blend until smooth.
2. Pulse to mix well and transfer the mixture evenly into mason jars.
3. Put the mason jars in the insert of Ninja Foodi and lock the lid.
4. Press "Bake/Roast" and bake for about 15 minutes at 360 degrees F.
5. Place in the refrigerator for 2 hours before serving and serve chilled.
- **Nutrition Info:** 244 calories, 24.8g fat, 2.1g carbs, 4g protein

www.ingramcontent.com/pod-product-compliance
Lightning Source LLC
Chambersburg PA
CBHW081418080526
44589CB00016B/2586